If Everyone Cared Enough

MARGARET TUCKER MBE

If Everyone Cared Enough

Her Voice Reclaimed

First Nations Peoples are advised this book contains depictions and names of deceased people, and content that may be considered culturally sensitive. The themes covered may also cause distress, and language that is not considered appropriate today is used in this book, reflecting the era in which it was first written.

This book is dedicated to my mother, Theresa Clements, who gave me a grounding in what is right as distinct from what is wrong. Many of the old people had this. I am grateful too for the practical training given by the white pioneers of the Murray-Murrumbidgee area towards the end of the last century and early this one. My mother's stories of those days have helped me to appreciate this wonderful country of ours, a God-given land that I hope many nationalities can share.

Margaret Tucker, 1977

We dedicate this new edition of our Nan's story to all First Nations mothers who have suffered the heartbreak of their children being taken from them, and also to the children who lost their families, culture, connection to country and their identities, for our Nanna Theresa was one of those mothers and our Nan Tucker was one of those children. We acknowledge and honour their spirit and strength to tell their stories to keep our culture and knowledge alive and strong for future generations.

Our nan would be very humbled today knowing that Australia has become a multicultural country and, in her words, 'it doesn't matter if you are black, white or brindle we all bleed the same colour'.

Love from Aunty Marge's Family, 2024

Foreword

Margaret 'Lilardia' Tucker MBE was a proud Yorta Yorta (Dhulinyagan) and Wiradjuri woman who devoted her life to civil rights and grassroots activism. She was affectionately known as Aunty Marge and Lilardia, her traditional Wiradjuri name, meaning 'flower'. Despite the adversity she faced as a survivor of the Stolen Generations, Aunty Marge remained dedicated to reconciliation and a better future for all Australians.

Aunty Marge's book had a profound effect on me when I first read it. It serves not only as a record of her own life but offers an important perspective on the lived experiences of many First Nations peoples. Her childhood memories of days spent playing with her cousins and learning from her Elders are brought to life through vivid recollection of their language, the games they played and the foods they ate. A section of the book that has now been carefully restored to its original state relays the stories Elders would tell to Aunty Marge. The stories are captured in great detail, including notes on how they were delivered to have the greatest impact. These stories, and the childhood recollections more generally, are an important record of Aunty Marge's culture as a Yorta Yorta and Wiradjuri woman.

When writing about being taken away from her family as a child, and being sent to the Cootamundra Domestic Training School for Aboriginal Girls, Aunty Marge is empathetic and forgiving. While she acknowledges how hard these times were on her and how it affected her and her family, Aunty Marge looks for the positives in even her worst experiences. Aunty Marge is generous in her account of the missionaries, teachers and families that were the driving forces behind these events, an example of the incredible strength of her character and kind nature.

Aunty Marge's original book was a valuable step towards the kind of truth-telling we look to embrace today, working towards reconciliation, and a deeper understanding of our shared histories. This edition is her truth and an important story to be heard by all Australians.

Without the vital work of people like Aunty Marge who had the courage to speak their truths, many Australians would still be completely unaware of the ongoing legacies of government policies and the Stolen Generations. This restored edition is yet another important step towards a more honest, respectful handling of our stories, told by our people.

The Hon Linda Burney MP
Minister for Indigenous Australians

Introduction

Yorta Yorta woman Margaret Tucker (1904–1996), fondly known as Aunty Marge, was one of the first Aboriginal authors to publish for mainstream Australian audiences. When her autobiography, *If Everyone Cared*, was released in 1977, her readers were largely unfamiliar with Aboriginal cultures and Aboriginal attitudes to Australia's settler invasion. With the needs and preferences of this envisaged audience in mind, significant changes were made to both the tone and content of the original manuscript, housed today in the National Library of Australia. Aunty Marge's original Aboriginal storytelling voice was altered. Political statements on the treatment of Aboriginal people were softened. Any colloquial Aboriginal English expressions that might have made Margaret Tucker look ill-educated or ignorant were deleted. Oral storytelling cues and genealogical information—elements that are important in Aboriginal cultures—were removed to avoid alienating audiences who couldn't imagine the Aboriginal cultural contexts evoked by Aunty Marge in her manuscript, like yarning around the fire. Her religious views were also softened, reducing statements that more liberal readers might have considered 'old-fashioned' moralisation.

The cumulative impact of these editorial decisions was significant, especially from the perspective of today, yet Aunty Marge willingly agreed to the re-fashioning of her manuscript and was thrilled when her book was released. Her schooling at segregated Aboriginal schools in rural New South Wales had left her with the impression that she was 'not too brainy' and a little in awe of white friends with lofty qualifications.[1] She was a survivor of racist government policies, including inferior education and forced child removal. She commenced her writing project as a sixty-nine-year-old with significant family and community responsibilities but with a growing public profile, a strong support network and clear motivation: a published autobiography would alert settler Australians to Aboriginal experience while also opening new and unique opportunities.

Aunty Marge was the first Aboriginal woman appointed to the Victorian Aborigines Welfare Board (1964) and later a representative to the Commonwealth Ministry of Aboriginal Affairs (1968). Associates began to urge Margaret Tucker to write down her life story after she was made a Member of the Order of the British Empire (Civil) in 1968, in recognition of her service to the Commonwealth. Members of the Aborigines Welfare Board backed these suggestions in the early 1970s by providing funding to support the writing project. Buoyed by such encouragement, Aunty Marge looked to close friends and fellow travellers in the Moral Re-Armament (MRA) organisation, Jean Hughes and Anne Ross, to help her realise the vision.[2] Chapter fourteen of *If Everyone Cared Enough* describes a life-changing encounter in 1956 that convinced Margaret Tucker to join this multifaith religious movement and led to her friendship with Hughes and Ross.

Moral Re-Armament, a worldwide movement dedicated to spiritual and ethical reawakening, was founded by an American Lutheran, Frank Buchman, in 1938. As the world was re-arming for a second world war, Buchman launched a campaign for moral and

1. Margaret Tucker, *If Everyone Cared Enough* (Canberra: NLA Publishing, 2024), p.86

2. Jennifer Jones, *Black Writers White Editors: Episodes of Collaboration and Compromise in Australian Publishing History* (Melbourne: Australian Scholarly Publishing, 2009), p.121

spiritual re-armament that he hoped would circumvent armed conflict.[3] The movement commonly used storytelling techniques including high-impact personal testimony, live theatre and film, to encourage individuals to take moral responsibility for their behaviour. In an age where structural sexism, racism and class-based limitation was common, MRA taught that all humans are equal irrespective of race, class or gender. They also endorsed four key ideals that they viewed as absolute values: honesty, purity, unselfishness and love. MRA sought to change the wider community by mobilising the power of apology and reparation, so converts were encouraged to acknowledge their wrongdoings publicly.[4] Individual change prompted by such public action, in turn, aided conflict resolution, reconciliation and social progress.[5] For example, in colonial Kenya the 1955 apology of a British officer in charge of a Mau-Mau 'rehabilitation' camp has been linked to the cessation of hostilities in the war of independence (1952–1960). Unprompted, the officer admitted to brutality, racism, arrogance and selfishness. His apology was so 'unimagined and unheard of' that leading Mau-Mau detainees also converted to MRA ideals and entered negotiations to end the war.[6]

Aunty Marge's conversion to MRA also came after an unexpected apology. An upper-class white woman used a musical event as a platform to publicly apologise for the discriminatory treatment metered out to Aboriginal Australians since white invasion. This woman hailed from the class of white settlers who had engaged Aboriginal girls as domestic

---

3. The campaign involved holding meetings that drew influential attendees at East Ham Town Hall, London, in 1938, and in New York, Washington, D.C., and California in 1939. Moral Re-armament Records, MSS56671, Manuscript Division, Library of Congress, Washington, D.C., USA.

4. Garth Lean, *Frank Buchman: A Life* (London: Constable and Company Limited, 1985)

5. Eric Dent and Craig Randall, 'Moral Re-Armament: Toward a Better Understanding of the Society-Corporation Relationship before the Emergence of 'Corporate Social Responsibility', *Journal of Management History* (2020)

6. Julius M. Gathogo, 'Nahashon Ngare Rukenya and the Moral Re-Armament in Kenya: The Turning Point and the Post Mau-Mau War Reconstruction (1959–1970)', *Studia Historiae Ecclesiasticae 44*, no.2 (2018), p.6

servants. Her apology for racial discrimination and recognition of suffering had a deep impact upon Aunty Marge, whose experience as a member of the Stolen Generations is central to her autobiography (chapters 7–11). MRA's absolute moral position on personal behaviour also resonated with Margaret Tucker's memory of the loving but rigid expectations of the Old People and her experience of communal living on Yorta Yorta and Wiradjuri Country as a child. Aboriginal society is conservative, in the sense that the future sustainability of a community group living in harsh and fragile environments is 'conserved' by deviating as little as possible from traditional knowledge and custom. Aunty Marge was motivated to preserve her generational knowledge in her autobiography, devoting much of *If Everyone Cared Enough* (chapters 1–6) to recollections of Aboriginal community life and the wisdom of her Elders.

Aunty Marge met her friend Jean Hughes in 1957 at Mackinac Island, MRA's convention centre on Lake Huron, Michigan. Modelled on the British 'country house weekend', MRA conferences created transformative group dynamics that were central to the movement's reconciliation agenda. Distinguished and worthy representatives of government, industry, trade unions, media, education, religious organisations and minority groups were drawn together at stately venues in settings of exceptional beauty (such as Caux in Switzerland) for several days or even weeks. Conference programs struck an informal tone through convivial dining experiences and rostered domestic tasks that saw the rich and the poor, and former foes, all 'peeling potatoes and washing up' together in the kitchen. This structured camaraderie, combined with a schedule of charismatic speakers, achieved an unobtrusive form of 'spiritual persuasion', which encouraged openness to moral discovery, public confession and reconciliation.[7] Jean Hughes had been a successful finance industry professional but gave up her

7. Edward Luttwak, 'Franco-German Reconciliation: The Overlooked Role of the Moral Re-Armament Movement', in *Religion, the Missing Dimension of Statecraft*, ed. Douglas Johnston and Cynthia Sampson (Oxford: Oxford University Press, 1994), p.48

career to volunteer full-time for MRA, serving in India in the early 1950s and accompanying an Indian Member of Parliament to the 1957 conference. Although only one chapter of *If Everyone Cared Enough* directly concentrates upon Aunty Marge's life-changing affiliation with MRA (chapter 15), the content and tone of her whole autobiography was profoundly shaped by MRA perspectives and priorities.

The autobiography project commenced during a typically busy period of life for Aunty Marge. She was serving on the Victorian Government's Aboriginal Affairs Advisory Council (which operated from 1967–1975) and was also involved with the Victorian Aboriginal and Torres Strait Islander Women's Council, which she established with her sister Geraldine Briggs in the late 1960s. This influential forerunner of the National Council of Aboriginal and Islander Women (established in 1972) provided an avenue for Aboriginal women to lobby government for change in areas of specific concern, including health and childcare. Aunty Marge's leadership experience, extensive networks and social influence were also critical to the establishment of the Victorian Aboriginal Health Service in 1973. At home, she was providing support for her daughter Mollie Dyer and five children. Dyer was then establishing the much-needed Victorian Aboriginal Child Care Agency, for which Aunty Marge acted as patron. The Dyer family home was understandably full of activity, as Aunty Marge's granddaughter Maxine Barr recalled:

> *It was nothing [to have] fourteen, fifteen people stayin' at our three-bedroom Commission place in Broadmeadows! I always remember, we'd be asleep, and then we'd be 'top and tailing' with our siblings, on the floor on a mattress, or on the couch … The house was always full of people.*[8]

Prior to meeting Aunty Marge, MRA friends Jean Hughes and Anne Ross, both middle-class white women, had no direct relationships with Aboriginal people. Witnessing the constant bubble of activity in

8. Maxine Barr, interview with Jennifer Jones

the extended-family home during their visits to Broadmeadows 'threw a lot of light' on Aunty Marge's life for the pair. Anne Ross recalled:

> *It was a fairly interesting experience* [visiting] *this place. Getting to know her family, getting to know the next-door neighbours, who were extended family, getting to know all the people who called in and out … Everybody who came; no one was refused anything. People would come and ask for help. She would listen to them and find out the whole story.*[9]

Maxine Barr also saw how busy her grandmother was in this period:

> *With all the fundraising and all the organisations, groups and stuff that she was in, all the committees she was on, she was inundated with people all the time. She would never have been able to write her book in her flat, never.*[10]

Hughes and Ross recognised that Aunty Marge's autobiographical project would benefit from access to a quiet space where she could write. The pair offered the use of a room in their home; first in Traralgon where Anne Ross was a general practitioner, and then in Camberwell after her retirement. They also took Aunty Marge on trips back to Yorta Yorta Country to stimulate recollections and, as the project concluded, organised a final writing retreat at Eildon Weir. Throughout this process, Jean Hughes encouraged Margaret Tucker to check her draft manuscript against MRA values:

> *Together they would go over what Marge has been writing … Jean was determined that it should be what Marge really wanted to say. She would often say when something would come up, some issue, 'now Marge is that what you really want say?' and Marge being an honest person would say 'Well no, no' and they would work at it to see what she had here* [gestures] *in her heart. Then they would try again until they got it right and that* [was] *what went into the book.*[11]

This checking process enabled the pair to identify 'issues' in the

9. Anne Ross, interview with Jennifer Jones

10. Maxine Barr, interview with Jennifer Jones

11. Anne Ross, interview with Jennifer Jones

manuscript that did not align with what Aunty Marge 'really wanted to say' in her book. Aunty Marge was a genuine MRA affiliate. MRA beliefs and practises had helped her to shed a debilitating suspicion of white people, resentment founded upon a lifetime of abusive treatment. Aunty Marge was deeply thankful when she found liberation from habitual responses to painful childhood memories and ongoing racial injustices. This gratitude for and acceptance of MRA teaching is reflected in the title of her autobiography, which abbreviates a motto of MRA founder Frank Buchman: 'If everyone cared enough and everyone shared enough, wouldn't everyone have enough?' Aunty Marge's autobiography is peppered with sayings that remind and encourage MRA adherents like herself to emulate the values of the movement in daily life.

Another MRA practise that profoundly shaped this autobiography is a meditation technique, known as 'guidance', which encourages habits of self-reflection and behavioural change.[12] Each morning, believers still themselves in order to hear the voice of God and to gain 'guidance' for daily action. Aunty Marge wrote her daily narrative of God's 'guidance' in notebooks that she kept specifically for this task. When beginning her autobiography, she simply expanded this daily writing practise to incorporate guidance on the contents of the book. It seems likely to me that this process included Aunty Marge practising selective recollection and self-censorship, which was then followed by Jean Hughes' edits, the pair cooperating to get the manuscript 'right'. This process shouldn't be interpreted as a form of narrative violence or an unwanted suppression; Aunty Marge shared the religious views of her friend and willingly reinterpreted her early life from the perspective of her late-adulthood beliefs. Neither was Aunty Marge a dupe to cultish religion. Although relatively obscure today, MRA was recognised globally after the Second World War and gained increasing influence as the cold war intensified.[13] MRA positioned itself as a mainstream movement capable of inspiring

12. Luttwak, op. cit., p.37

13. The MRA organisation changed its name to 'Initiatives of Change' in 2001.

transformative world change, offering both a viable alternative to communism and a set of multifaith religious morals that could shore up the reconstruction of society.[14]

Narrative decisions made by Aunty Marge and Jean Hughes had a clear impact upon the autobiography's focus. Aunty Marge's formative political experiences as a young adult in Melbourne were heavily censored. Her leading role as an Aboriginal activist who found support and understanding from union organisers and communists—including a 1935 appearance in newsreel film funded by the Communist Party of Australia titled A Princess of an Ancient Tribe—receive passing attention or are left out entirely. As a founding member of the Aboriginal Advancement League, and an organiser of the 1938 National Day of Mourning alongside Pastor Doug Nicholls and William Cooper, Aunty Marge had developed 'close personal connections' with leading left-wing Melbournians in the interwar period. These friends included Trades Hall leader George Franks and his wife, who are likely the unnamed 'Communist friends' who took Aunty Marge into their home when she was otherwise destitute.[15] She later acknowledged the pair in the 1983 documentary film *Lousy Little Sixpence*, perhaps because the social taint of communism had decreased and the social standing of Aboriginal activists and their allies had increased. Other omissions from the book, however, resulted from edits to Aunty Marge's original manuscript. The role played by Helen Baillie, a high-society nurse and Christian Socialist, for example, is described in the manuscript but obscured in the first edition of *If Everyone Cared*.[16]

Baillie had formed the Aboriginal Fellowship Group with like-minded white Christians in 1931 and joined the Victorian Aboriginal

---

14. Dent and Randall, op. cit.

15. Heather Goodall, *Invasion to Embassy* (Sydney: Allen and Unwin, 1996), p.230; Margaret Tucker, Manuscript, MS 8704, National Library of Australia (Tucker, 2024, op. cit., p.163).

16. Patricia Grimshaw and Peter Sherlock, 'One Woman's Concerns for Social Justice: The Letters of Helen Baillie to Farnham Maynard, 1933–1936', in *Anglo-Catholicism in Melbourne: Papers to Mark the 150th Anniversary of St Peter's Eastern Hill 1846–1996*, ed. Colin Holden (Parkville, Vic.: University of Melbourne, Department of History, 1997), p.88

Group in 1933, to pursue social justice through practical assistance and lobbying. Unlike George Franks, who Aunty Marge chooses to recall but not to name in her manuscript, Helen Baillie is mentioned several times by name in the original hand-written text. Here she is acknowledged as 'one of the genuine ones' who 'gave up her time, her home, and her life for Aboriginal people' and 'did not expect honours or glory for it'.[17] Helen Baillie drove William Cooper, Margaret Tucker and Doug Nicholls to Sydney for the Aboriginal Day of Mourning on 26 January 1938, 'when white Australia celebrated 150 years of history'.[18] Baillie also provided regular material support during the Cummeragunja Walk-Off of 1939, which saw residents of the NSW Cummeragunja Aboriginal Station take strike action by crossing the Murray River to live in Victoria, in protest of poor living conditions and abusive treatment.[19] Baillie drove supplies from Melbourne to Barmah with Anton Vroland on behalf of Melbourne-based Aboriginal welfare organisations.[20] The Christian foundation of Baillie's social justice activism may have prompted Aunty Marge to detail her contribution in the original manuscript. Perhaps the details were later deleted from the first edition because Baillie's socialist-leanings did not meet MRA approval. She is given a veiled role in *If Everyone Cared*, appearing as an unnamed 'white woman' who helped foster Aunty Marge's 'work for my people'.[21]

Although Aunty Marge clearly intended her autobiography to play a role in 'consciousness-raising' efforts that would educate white Australians about Aboriginal culture and Aboriginal historic experience, any overt political statement on the treatment of Aboriginal people or criticism of white people's ignorance was minimised to avoid offence. In chapter one of the manuscript, for example, Aunty Marge reflects

17. Tucker, Manuscript, op. cit. (Tucker, 2024, op. cit., p.166).

18. Grimshaw and Sherlock, op. cit.

19. See Richard Broome, *Aboriginal Victorians: A History since 1800* (Crows Nest, NSW: Allen & Unwin, 2005), p.262–264

20. 'WHY BLACKS LEFT: Meeting at Camp', *Argus*, 27 February 1939, p2

21. Tucker, *If Everyone Cared* (Sydney: Ure Smith, 1977), p.164

upon neglectful government administrations that allowed whole Aboriginal families to die of pneumonia and tuberculosis. They treated Aboriginal people like 'a blot, a big dirty blot on an uncaring sort of administration'.[22] Aunty Marge's aim was to help her readers to understand how discriminatory treatment felt from an Aboriginal point of view. In the manuscript, she suggests:

> *Colour is not the most important issue; people are! When one is called such names as 'half-breed' ... while I am not bitter about it, I feel this story of mine may help not only our dark youths of today but white people to see the real us! The human feelings of Aborigines, even now, are mostly not understood. Not even by our wonderful white friends!*[23]

Here Aunty Marge identifies the culpability of white people, even the sympathetic ones. The published first edition of *If Everyone Cared*, however, strikes a different tone:

> *When one is called half-caste, one feels very bitter. But I believe this story of mine may help both our dark youths of today and white people too, to see the real causes of the so-called Aboriginal problem. It may help both sides to understand each other better.*[24]

Here Aunty Marge is 'very bitter' about her past treatment, and implies that Aboriginal people need to make as much effort to foster cross-racial understanding as white people do. Deflecting the overt criticism of white people limits Aunty Marge's capacity to communicate her unique perspective.

The translation of her colloquial Aboriginal English into Standard English also substantially reduces the character of the original autobiography. Small alterations mute Aunty Marge's 'yarning' voice and make key episodes in her story much less impactful. When thirteen-year-old Margaret Tucker has been sent from Cootamundra Domestic Training Home for Aboriginal Girls into service, she finds herself alone in Sydney facing the unrealistic expectations of her new white mistress.

22. Tucker, Manuscript, op. cit. (Tucker, 2024, op. cit., p.20).

23. Ibid (Tucker, 2024, op. cit., p.21).

24. Tucker, 1977, op. cit., p.30

The manuscript reads:

> *Now I was on my own in this big city with white people whom I had never lived with before. A deep loneliness settled on me. I was scared for the first time.*
>
> *I realised we were dressed in things that made us look older than we were. I realised that a lot would be expected of me now. But it was a sham! I did not know the first thing about the way white people lived.*[25]

In the published version, the culpability of government administrators—who sent under-prepared Aboriginal children to do the work of adults—is minimised, and Aunty Marge's declaration that 'it was a sham!' is deleted:

> *I was on my own in this big city with white people who I had never lived with before. A deep loneliness settled on me. I was scared for the first time. Although I did not know the first thing about the way white people lived, I began to realise a lot would be expected of me.*[26]

Editorial strategies, like removing colloquial language, were likely implemented with good intentions. In the 1970s, 'Standard English' (the variety taught in schools and used for official and legal purposes) served as the benchmark for proper communication. Standard English was still perceived to be 'more correct, precise, pure and elegant' than Australian English, which was often 'dismissed as an inappropriate and inferior variety'.[27] Aboriginal English held even less status. Changes that now seem to have impeded Aunty Marge's Aboriginal storytelling style were probably designed to protect her prestige.

The perceived low value of Aboriginal cultural expression also impacted elements of *If Everyone Cared* that were directed at Aboriginal audiences rather than white readers. Although Aunty Marge makes clear that her autobiography was intended for both the 'dark youths of today and white people too', the needs of the non-Aboriginal readership are

25. Tucker, Manuscript, op. cit. (Tucker, 2024, op. cit., p.105).

26. Tucker, 1977, op. cit., p.106

27. Jennifer Price, 'New News Old News: A Sociophonetic Study of Spoken Australian English in News Broadcast Speech', *AAA: Arbeiten aus Anglistik und Amerikanistik 33*, no.2 (2008), p.285–286

sometimes prioritised. Details that seemed unimportant from a white person's perspective, like kinship information and cues from the oral tradition, were deleted from the book. In the manuscript, Aunty Marge opened chapter three by explaining: 'I am doing my best to relay stories handed down in my family—handed down for seven generations in a very natural way'. She then relates two of the 'blood curdling stories we loved to hear' around the campfire when she was a child: the first about a frightening old woman who stole Aboriginal children from their mothers; and the second about the 'Beccers', part-human and part-animal creatures that also stole and ate unwary Aboriginal children. These performances were 'stage-managed' by oral cues that gain and maintain listener/reader attention. Aunty Marge explained:

> *The old people would open their tales with a sound that went 'o-o-o-oh', with a rising inflection that immediately commanded our attention.*[28]

Having opened the chapter by indicating that she is actively preserving both the storytelling method and the content of the tales, Aunty Marge presents both stories using the method she had just described—now translated into written form. Oral cues, for example, announce key twists in the plot:

> *Well then, 'ooooh', all the hunters came back to the camp.*[29]

Aunty Marge also uses a mid-story 'dramatic aside' to address her readership. This technique includes her imagined audience in the intimate atmosphere of the campfire and strengthens the author–reader bond. Describing the Beccer creatures, who have acute hearing and a sharp sense of smell, she notes with a wry effect:

> *the soles of their feet were very tender, and their eyes, which were small and red, were very weak. (Well, we cannot have everything all the time, can we.)*[30]

This aside uses humour to break the rising tension and to remind the reader of Aunty Marge's role as a narrator who is sharing her generational

---

28. Tucker, Manuscript, op. cit. (Tucker, 2024, op. cit., p.42).

29. Ibid (Tucker, 2024, op. cit., p.43).

30. Ibid (Tucker, 2024, op. cit., p.13).

knowledge with them. At the conclusion of the two stories, an oral cue marks the end of the performance:

> *Wee-ee-eeoh! Uttered in a descending note; is a typical ending of stories from the old people.*[31]

Confusingly, the first edition of *If Everyone Cared* removes some of these oral cues and retains others. Aunty Marge's framing rationale for the chapter, which carefully positions her written text in the Aboriginal oral tradition, is deleted, as are the oral cues that contextualise the first tale about the frightening old woman. The second traditional story about the Beccers, however, retains the oral staging, perhaps because it is more obviously 'mythological'. But the dramatic aside is also removed: a treatment that diminishes the corporeal presence of Aunty Marge as a storyteller and reduces the overall cultural coherence of her book.

Other indicators of a distinctive Aboriginal world view were also altered to better suit the conventions of the Western autobiographical genre. Aunty Marge's original manuscript is not chronological; it does not adopt the conventional birth-to-success narrative trajectory that is characteristic of most life writing. Instead, the manuscript is thematic and circular, beginning on significant Aboriginal land at Moonahcullah, where Aunty Marge spent her early childhood, and ending at Black's Mountain, an important cultural site, where Theresa Clements first felt her baby, Margaret, kick in the womb. This ordering reiterates the importance of community, Country and inherited knowledge, rather than competition and individual achievement—as is usually the case in Western autobiography. Margaret Tucker intended the concluding section of chapter sixteen, which was deleted from the first edition, to focus on the living wisdom passed down from her grandmother 'who could hardly speak English and worked for a bit of tucker'. This wisdom was passed to Theresa Clements, then to Margaret, and now to readers everywhere. Affirming the oral tradition as a foundation for contemporary living, Aunty Marge concludes her manuscript by writing:

31. Tucker, Manuscript, op. cit. (Tucker, 2024, op. cit., p.47).

> *I say what my old mother used to say: 'don't feel sorry for yourselves, be up and doing'. Let us get together, black and white, people from all over the world care and share for humanity in the way God means us to care and share.*[32]

The published first edition instead closes with a popular African-American saying (attributed to musician Benny Goodman) that aligns with MRA philosophy,

> *You can play a tune of sorts on the white keys of a piano; you can play a tune of sorts on the black keys; but for perfect harmony, you must use both.*[33]

This new edition of Margaret Tucker's landmark autobiography heeds her original exhortation to 'be up and doing' something positive. Closely following the original handwritten manuscript as a guide, the following chapters repatriate Aunty Marge's Aboriginal English. Small but frequent changes restore her generous storytelling voice, inviting readers into a close author–reader relationship that she believed could heal misunderstanding. Aunty Marge's stories communicate cultural priorities and political views that were removed from the original publication. Come and sit around Aunty Marge's campfire and hear the stories that she wanted to pass down, told in her own voice, and in print for the first time.

32.Tucker, Manuscript, op. cit. (Tucker, 2024, op. cit., p.207).

33. Tucker, *If Everyone Cared*, op. cit., p.205

If Everyone Cared Enough

Chapter One

My two friends recently took me for a delightful visit to Deniliquin and then to Moonahcullah, both my childhood haunts. We stayed in a motel on the banks of the Edward River, which was very high and wide at that point. It seems silly to say, but my heart filled with gladness because it was a beautiful sight, and my two friends loved it. We were given a room in that motel where one could just lie in bed, pull the blind away and see the old river flowing. On those same banks my mother had camped as a child.

We went to visit Old Morago homestead, where my mother had worked when I was small and where we had played with her boss's children, with no division between black and white. Nor was there any when I visited on this occasion. The dear old homestead is over a hundred years old now. The old mulberry tree that we Aboriginal children shared with the boss's children: one of the young Eastman boys fell down from this tree and broke his arm. He was rushed to Deniliquin hospital. He did not want anyone to go with him or hold him except my mother.

After having a cup of tea with the Eastman daughters and talking over old times, I crossed the Edward River to the place where Moonahcullah once stood. My first glimpse of the place was of the few remaining fences and, through an old gate, the cemetery a little further beyond. Most of the graves neatly marked with wooden crosses and artificial flowers. After looking at the names on the crosses, I could not find the old familiar names that I had remembered were buried when I was a girl. So, I asked my friend who had come with us from her home in Deniliquin. She pointed to an old pepper tree where masses of weeds were high and cattle were grazing. My heart ached at those forgotten graves, and I felt that in a couple of hundred years the bones of our relations will be dug up for experimental purposes, the rest-in-peace crosses long rotted away. I am told by old Uncle Billy Day's grandson that they are going to clean it up and I do hope so.

As I remembered that cemetery at old Moonahcullah, where I first went to school in a bough shed, and the other one at Cummeragunja, my heart ached. I thought that soon they won't even be a memory, those grand old warriors, every one of them the original pioneers of this country for thirty thousand years. As the tears rolled down my cheeks, I remembered my old mother, called the last remaining Queen of the Ulupna tribe of Murray River. Like a lot of our dear old people of that district, the older women were called 'Yarmuk', meaning Mother, Aunty or relation. Well, as I gazed at the place where they slept underground I felt at least they are at peace, and I fancied I could hear my mother's voice saying to me, like of old, 'Stop feeling sorry and miserable for the bygone days, be up and doing something worthwhile'. Lots of our old people thought that way too, but wondered how, and which way to begin. We had to learn the white man's language if we wished to exist. To make matters worse, down this end of Australia, we lost our own language and our identity in becoming light-skinned.

Moonahcullah was an Australian Inland Mission settlement or reserve, and it was here that I was brought up, in a mud-brick hut partitioned off to make sleeping quarters. A bark roof, lined inside with hessian, the walls papered.

Although the huts were small with earthen floors, these homes were kept clean. Oh, there were about four or five weatherboard homes

Old Morago homestead, where Margaret's mother worked.

built by the government, no lining. They were cold in the winter and hot in summer.

My mother's father, George Middleton, was one of three light-skinned babies born in a tribe. They had to be kept near their mothers for fear of them being spirited away. They were about three years of age before the tribe accepted them. It came to my mind that we, in our early days, discriminated against another colour too. I thank God for helping me to see that 'people are people' and it is not colour that matters, but character.

My grandfather could not read or write, but he had a longing to have a farm of his own. With the help of some of the white farmers around, who lent him equipment, he cleared some bushland, which he bought. I was told he farmed it successfully and then sold it to a white farmer. He bought a bigger piece of land, which he put all his heart into. It was just a mile away from the mission, Cummeragunja, where his wife and children stayed, the children going to school. His only son died, so his name died with him, but he had three daughters who helped him. I can remember my mother telling us that after her mother died, they used to dig rabbit burrows, work with the horses that pulled the plough and chaff cutter, as well as cleaning and washing. Grandfather always had them help in the busy farm times, even after they were married, but then my mother and her younger sister got sick of farm work, so they ran away to a neighbouring Aboriginal reserve. I might say my mother and her sister Christina ran away to Warangesda, near Darlington Point on the Murrumbidgee River, which is 300 kilometres from Cummeragunja! The reserve has long since been abolished and the land sold. It was here my mother met and married Bill Clements and I was born.

Grandfather Middleton was a very stern old man, but me and my younger sisters spent many happy holidays at his farm while my mother cooked for him and his farm hands, who were Aboriginal men and relations from the mission. I will always remember the fig pies and jam Mother made. Grandfather had a small orchard of figs growing near the farmhouse. The trees were so thick with leaves you could not see the sky through the foliage. But, oh my, our mouths would be sore from eating figs—in spite of mother telling us not to eat the skin!

We children loved to take the lovely lunch of fig jam tart and meat pie out into the sandhills where the men and Grandfather were digging out rabbit warrens. When they were full in the breeding seasons, we children would watch them dig to the end of the burrow, pull the struggling bunnies out, and exterminate them amid our cries of horror and anger. But once when they pulled out some baby rabbits, we begged to nurse them for a little while. Holding the furry little animal, so cuddlesome and lovable, was too much for me. So, I sneaked away with it. I was halfway back to the farmhouse when the men missed it. I looked back and saw the men waving to me to bring that little bunny back, so I ran squealing to the farmhouse, bringing my mother and aunt running towards me. They thought something awful had happened to one of the children. I explained the situation to them, and they said my grandfather would deal with me, but he didn't, although he was a stern man.

I was twenty-one years of age when he died. I was at his bedside. I had a great deal of respect and love for this quiet old man with the long snowy white beard. He died in a tent, my mother caring for him, at the age of about eighty-five years. He preferred the tent, 'plenty fresh air', he said. I felt that he was a very lonely old man.

I can remember our only amusement being the pictures in this small town of Barham. One Saturday night, my cousin, Jack Patten, aged twenty, tried his luck in asking the old grandfather if he would shout us to the pictures. We others were too afraid to ask him. He wouldn't even buy himself the best food the whole time that he was ill, and my mother had to scrounge the right kind of food. So, Grandfather asked Jack to go get his Bible and read a few verses—what's more, the old man made us all sit around and listen. Jack didn't bite the old man for money (ask for a loan) again! However, Grandfather left his three daughters a few thousand each when he died. He was buried at Cummeragunja on the beloved Murray River near his wife and only son, and later his daughter, my mother.

Chapter One

My old aunt, my mother's oldest sister, died a lonely death in the Deniliquin hospital, none of us being near. My old uncle is buried in Barham, in his beloved part of the country, Koondrook/Kerang districts, where a lot of his ancestors died thousands of years before him. He told us, also his old Brother-Uncle Billy Ingram told us where the burial grounds were, but they were never to be revealed. I can remember old Uncle Billy threatening a white man who used to dig for the skeletons of our people, to sell to the museum. The white man was scared stiff of Uncle Billy's threat. He did not dig there about anymore. So, it was with mixed feelings that I read in the papers recently about fossil remains, over thirty thousand years old, in a swamp. Some of our Aboriginal people made a fuss about the bones being disturbed. We on the Advisory Council of the Ministry for Aboriginal Affairs were shown a film about the digging. Actually, I felt great awe in watching that film shown in colour and explained in detail by the curator of the museum, whom I have a great deal of respect and liking for. I did not agree with a lot of what he said, but I guess he was doing his job. I feel no matter where they rest, let them rest in peace.

My mother's English name was Theresa Priscilla Middleton; her Aboriginal name died with her. White people called them these names because Aboriginal names were too hard for them to pronounce. My mother was married to William Clements, called Bill, in a Catholic Church in Gundagai, fourteen miles from Brungle where our Aboriginal reserve was situated and on which my father's mother lived at the time. My grandmother had six children that I know of. She was just on six feet tall and full blood. I see the church where Mother and Father were married every time I travel by car or bus to Canberra or Sydney. It is a joy to see the Murrumbidgee River, where I was born. I was registered in Hay in 1904, so was my younger sister Geraldine Rose, born in 1910. Two other sisters, May Edna and Evelyn Louise, were born on the Murray River. May died about twenty years ago, before my mother. She took the life of our people so much to heart. It is a long story, which I may say something about, but not much because it is her story.

She will not mind me saying something positive that may help bring understanding of our people's indignities and struggles.

May and Evelyn were born at Cummeragunja. May was the second to me, then Evelyn, then Geraldine. Four girls all within six years, no wonder my father went shearing and roaming and we did not see him for five years. He was a fine stamp of a man and, in a way, we were proud of him. During the prime of his life he was chosen with the other coloured people to act in some of Oscar Asche's plays. I was twenty-one years then. Peter Felix, Edgar Bux and other well-known coloured singers and boxers were part of that group. Peter Felix was half an inch taller than my father, who was six feet five inches. I remember him acting in Oscar Asche's plays *Chu Chin Chow* and *Cairo*.

My father's people roamed around where the Murrumbidgee flowed, long before Canberra was thought of. His people used to camp at the foot of what was called Blacks' Mountain, now it is called Black Mountain. Now white people use it as a caravan park. The first time I visited (this will sound strange, but not so strange) my father's mother, old Granny Bedgie, took my mother, then her new daughter-in-law, camping around her tribal territory. That was three months before I was born. As long as I live, I will always visualise what Canberra looked like before that beautiful city and lake were there. Please forgive me, but I am so proud of my country and of being an Aboriginal Australian.

Father was not well in health and Mother went to help nurse him in his last days. He wanted me to go over to see him and bring my little girl, but times were hard, so we could not make the trip to Sydney. I long to visit his grave, I feel he must have been lonely. He was buried at Rookwood cemetery in Sydney.

I have already told of Father's absence for years at a time. He was a roamer. Then he came home to see us, after being away five years. He was like a stranger, but the short while he was with us, we learned to respect him, to love him and to hold no animosity towards him. My youngest sister had been a baby when he left the five years ago, so she did not know what it was like to call a man 'Dad'. We had plenty of uncles and

Chapter One

May, Margaret, Geraldine, Theresa and Evelyn (clockwise from left).

cousins, in fact everyone was Uncle and Cousin and Aunty—especially if we wanted something.

Father would play ball with us sometimes, throwing it to each of us. The little sister would call to him, 'Throw it to me now, man'. This happened several times until our father got a bit hurt and annoyed. He stopped the game, gathered us around him. He put his arm around the little sister and said to us all, 'I am your father, don't call me "man". In future, call me Dad'. He especially looked at our little sister and said to her, 'You are my little baby girl and I am your dad. It is wrong to say, "here man, give me the ball"'.

So, we started playing with the ball again and the little sister got excited and called to him again, saying 'man'. He pretended not to hear her, then she remembered and said hesitatingly, 'Man-Da-Dad'. He picked her up, hugged her and gave her the ball. It was 'Dad' from then on.

The nearest big town to Moonahcullah was twenty-five miles away—Deniliquin. Some lucky family might have a buggy drawn by one or two horses, or perhaps they were unlucky, as it would be borrowed by the rest of the community. It would be loaned reluctantly, or not very eagerly, but in the case of illness never refused. You can imagine the difficulties, travelling twenty-five miles with buggy and horse on miles of boggy roads, mud up to your axles. Most times a horse pulling through that boggy road would be dead-beat, needing lots of rest. You would be lucky to arrive at your destination within two or three days. However, it was an adventure, and we loved it.

Sometimes the police from Deniliquin would visit the reserve. It was part of their work. We would see their shiny helmets coming around the river bend. As soon as we spotted them, we children would dive under a bed or run for the lagoon which was joined to the river. The growth of shrubs made good hiding places. It was not only the children who were afraid of the police. No doubt there were some good fellows among them, but we had reason to believe that any contact with anyone in those uniforms was not good for us. Even if a grown-up was spoken to by the police, they would 'see nothing, say nothing, hear nothing'.

Chapter One

One day, three Aboriginal children walking along the road which ran by the riverbank, chatting happily, did not notice the horse and rider until he was right near them. The policeman looked down at them from his horse and observed their stony faces.

'Hello', he says to them, but their gaze is on the ground, not looking to right or left.

One girl is twelve years of age, the other eleven, and the boy about the same age.

'Hello', the policeman says again. No answer, the three youths still walking along, looking at the ground.

Policeman tries again: 'Is so-and-so at the mission?' (meaning the Blacks' Camp).

No answer.

'Has he been drunk and playing up?'

Still no answer, walking along, heads down.

The policeman raises his voice angrily, 'If you don't answer me, I'll lock up the three of you. Now answer me,' he repeats his question.

The three children look at each other with wild frightened eyes. A quick look at the horse—no, they couldn't outrun it. Then they look up at the policeman. The youngest girl clutches the older and tries to hide behind her.

'Oh, I can see I can't get anything out of you,' the policeman says gruffly.

So, whenever they saw the policeman's helmet shining in the distance, the children would run for the bush and the lagoon.

Summertime, every day we were down at the river swimming. Our parents would not let us go swimming until the shade from the trees that grew along the riverbank was over the water. Old Aunt and Mother explained that with the rest of our bodies in the water, the hot sun would beat down on the back of our heads and cause us to be sunstruck. That is what it was called by our people. We children were not very happy with that arrangement, but our old folks were very strict about it.

One weekend, we older kids made up our minds to go up the river, hot sun glaring down on us. We were like ducks; we loved the water. Our ages ranged from about six to thirteen or a bit more—boys and girls. It was a natural happening. Bigger ones would usually wear long dresses, but none of us had thoughts of these things as we sneaked up the river, where our parents could not stop us from swimming. We were so hot. We all peeled off our clothes and the wonderful feeling when our hot little bodies hit the water, the squeals of delight. Time was forgotten, seeing who could keep underwater the longest, or who could swim the farthest under water, throwing objects into the deepest parts of the water and retrieving them, diving from the limbs of trees that were overhanging the river. We forgot that sounds carry a long way, and that the old aunt would be looking for one of us to fetch a bucket of water for her in a cleaned-out kerosene tin used for water vessels.

When no-one answered her call, she went to the river herself, so as she got her water, she heard our joyous shouts and screams afar. It really was a boiling hot day and she was very cross. As she started walking up the river towards us brown water children, her eyes were angry at the thought of us daring to disobey her, swimming and risking sunstroke in the middle of the day. Oh my, she was spotted about a hundred yards or so through the scrub by one of the youths. All of us rushed out of the river, gathering our clothes as we ran. Some picked up the wrong clothes. I can even see it clearly now, some of the bigger boys hopping along on one leg trying to put their pants on. The girls with our hair dripping, looking like something drowned that had been dragged out of the water.

You can imagine about twenty of us in our native state, and one elderly black woman, who had a long green switch in her hand, and she did not spare the rod. The hot sun did not cool her anger, especially when she saw some of the boys and girls whom she said 'should know better'. The boys, as they got older, were graded out of mixed bathing unless both lots of older ones wore knickers and dresses. However, we were punished, we were not allowed to go swimming, no matter how hot. We could cool off by splashing or having a turn in those large old galvanised tubs, either borrowed or owned.

We girls had well-kept heads of curly hair, which was a misery sometimes. Mother and Aunt would go through our heads with a fine-tooth comb, and then part it bit by bit to see if there was anything in it that should not be. We would beg them to finish, as we wanted to play, but to no avail.

There was a lovely sandy spot situated about half a mile from the Aboriginal reserve. This spot was a creek or swamp-like; it was mostly dry unless floods came and filled all these places up. There were fallen trees and huge dried-up logs, shrubs and quite a lot of wildlife, including rabbits and snakes. Our parents would not allow we children to explore there, mostly because of the snakes.

But some of our parents, my mother especially, liked to wash on the bed of this dry creek, jutting out from a sheltered bend of the Edward River. There was plenty of wood to boil the white towels and clothes, heating up the water in old kerosene tins that made great utensils. Three or four parents would have washday there and, what's more, they would allow us to strip off and take a piece of soap and wash our younger sisters or brothers. Our hair and little black bodies would be shining. Only the soles of our feet and hands were white. I know white people find this a source of wonderment.

We would get up to a lot of fun and frolic in the water, seeing who could dive the farthest, then swimming to and fro across the river. We would put our little sisters or brothers on our backs, crawling on our hands and knees, pretending to be a horse. With my little sister on my back, I pretended to buck. Anyway, it was a little too realistic and my little sister, aged four, was unseated. The next thing I saw was two legs sticking up in the air and her head under water. When I got over my shock, I grabbed her and pulled her up. Then I saw my mother's terrified face. She had a big stick in her hand to wallop me, and a wild look in her eyes. My little sister was trying to rub hair and sand out of her eyes. I felt little sister was safe enough now, but I wasn't! I had to think quickly. I swam for safety into deep waters, until we were almost ready to go home. Then, very helpfully, I gathered the dry clothes from the bushes (really good drying places), helping my mother, but keeping an eye on her in case! However, all was forgotten and forgiven as we carried our clean washing home.

This sandy swimming spot and washing place was handy for us all, because our parents would have a swim too, before going home. It would be great fun for we pang-pang gooks. They would teach us to swim and we would all play games. They were truly happy times.

If the men were lucky enough to have a job on sheep stations, through the year they would buy two or three sheep between them with their wages. They would bring them home and share them with all the families. When a sheep was to be killed, all we children would be hunted away, only to return to beg for parts of the sheep. We were hungry and wanted to cook it on the coals right away!

Times were hard when there was a drought, with no benevolent societies around or social services in existence then. There were no luscious greens, the rivers were dry, so fish were scarce; wild ducks and swans went further afield. Emus and kangaroos were further away because fences had been built to keep them out. We children knew what it was to have empty tummies, although many times, in fact, I don't think our hungry cries for food were even heard. Sometimes a relation would come to light with a damper and, oh boy, slices with wild honey would be given to us pang-pang gooks. I can remember we kids making that slice of damper last as long as we could. I could never master that art. My sister in age next to me was never very strong, but she would always nibble her slice gently. As we were still hungry, we would watch her. She would break off a piece of her bread and honey to give us. Sometimes we would feebly say, 'Oh, no, we've had ours'. She would answer, 'I'm not very hungry'. She was always like that.

I do know sometimes the squatter would miss a few sheep, but as we were hungry, we devoured lamb stews, lamb grilled on the coals and soups. We children did not question where it came from; we knew we had to keep our mouths closed.

Some enterprising families had a few goats and they multiplied very fast. I remember them well because the boys and one or two adventurous girls would try to ride on their backs, only to be chased by the old billy goat with tremendous horns and long whiskers. But when the droughts came, they dwindled away—for want of food for goats and for people! I've not eaten goat since those hungry years, although I've had my hungry moments since.

Things were not so bad when Mother worked on neighbouring homesteads and stations. We would benefit from leftovers from the kitchen. She would walk miles from these places where she worked, back to our settlement. The aunt who helped rear us four sisters was my mother's sister. My uncle, her husband, was of the Wamba Wamba tribe. Mother and Aunt were born in the Murray River district.

We spent our childhood days between Moonahcullah on the Edward River at Old Maloga, where different tribes were brought together by the Reverend Matthews, to see how they would take to living in groups. Then they were all moved to Cummeragunja, across the river from Echuca. An Indian teacher was got from Mauritius, whom three generations of children loved. My mother couldn't speak a word of English when she first went to school, but at the age of sixteen she was an assistant teacher. My mother and aunt were from the Ulupna tribe—more about them later.

My mother and aunt spent long times at Cummeragunja, their home settlement. While Father was away shearing, Mother worked. He was sought after as a shearer in different states, so we didn't see a lot of him.

My younger sister, who was about two years or eighteen months at this time, stayed close to my aunt and uncle as they roamed about. I can remember being poled by dear old Granny Kate in a log canoe around Moira Lakes, an overflow from the Murray River. Our people often camped round the Moira Lakes, as there was a plentiful supply of fish in the season, swan and duck eggs.

My mother and aunt's tribe and many of the other tribes scattered around have now intermarried. I feel we are one big tribe together.

Earlier, each of our tribes had their own head men and women, who led their activities and gave advice. As far as I can remember, the women could hunt game as well as the men.

During the time we lived in Cummeragunja, I recall it was a happy environment. It had seemed to have progressed much more than Moonahcullah in living conditions. A cottage was given to our family to live in, or we would stay with relations, of which we had many. Then there was always our grandfather on the farm a mile away. Mother or Aunt would each go once or twice a week to wash and clean house for him when the farming season was slack. Of course, it was a great joy for we children to go along to play under the fig trees and around the sand-hills. But woe betide us if Grandfather found us trespassing around the property on our own. He felt we would be getting into mischief if we were not in the company of adults. One season when the work was a little slack and we stayed at the farm, our father happened to be helping Grandad and another Aboriginal man (half the size of my father) named Sandy Glass.

My mother always had a following of younger friends and friends her age, and on this day they all gave a hand in the cleaning and washing and finished early. Oh joy, we had homemade crayfish nets and little bits of meat saved for the occasion and all of us—Mother, my aunt, two or three eighteen-year-old girls and a number of children—climbed through the fences and made for a dam, which supplied drinking water for cattle, horses and sheep. It was called the Mission Paddock, about half a mile away from Cummeragunja and half a mile away from Grandad's farm.

It was a very hot day as we tramped across the ploughed field, it was rough going for the bare little feet. Mother had left our baby sister; she was then about eighteen months. She was sound asleep, and someone was at the farm. Mother said we would not be away for very long. However, crays (we called them crawfish) were plentiful in that dam and it was great fun. We learned the right way to catch them and they were delicious to eat. Mother said it was time to go back to the farm because the little sister may be awake. We climbed through the fence and the older group was a few yards ahead, because we had stopped to count how many yabbies we had caught. Like children, we discovered someone had pinched someone else's. Our second youngest sister was with us, she was three-and-a-half years old. One of the children happened to drop a crayfish and was just about to pick it up when almost all of us noticed the tiger snake lying right across our path. The bigger children jumped over it, others jumped away and ran around it, but the small sister tried to jump over it and the snake curled itself around her leg and bit her below her little knee. She screamed. I had forgotten she was with us; I ran back, only to find Mother was there before me. She picked up a big stick and struck the snake so hard she broke its back. But the stick broke too, and the snake was trying to strike mother. She got another stick lying nearby and killed the reptile. We were all crying for our little sister who was bitten. Mother, although weeping, told a couple of boys to run to the farmhouse, which fortunately we were near, to see if our father was at home. Fortunately, he was, and the other man, Sandy Glass. They broke all records as they ran to see what the matter was. We were all screaming and crying for little sister. Father took his boots off, so did the other man, and they pulled out the laces. Mother had hold of my sister's leg and was sucking out the poisonous blood for all she was worth. Father tied the bootlaces around the leg, two above and two below the wound. Then he and Sandy Glass ran across the ploughed field, jumping fences, taking short cuts, all of us following. Mother was running, her long black hair flying, then she stopped as she thought of her baby sleeping up at the farm alone. 'My baby is all alone at the farm—I must get her,' she gasped out. One of the women, long since gone to our last tribal sleeping place, said, 'I will fetch her, you go on'.

Cummeragunja was more advanced than many Aboriginal reserves, and it had a dispensary for nursing medicine and the doctor, whom we all respected and liked, visited the reserve every week. On the day the snake bit my sister, he happened to be there at the manager's house in the quarters where he examined the sick Aboriginal people.

Sometimes he could not come out. However, the Good Spirit sure does answer prayers and is merciful, because the doctor was right there. I can remember his name to this day—Dr Stoney of Echuca. He earned the entire gratitude of we Aboriginal people more times than I can remember. Also, his great helper, whom we looked upon as a doctor too. That was Mr Thomas James, our well-loved and respected Indian teacher, who helped and learned how to mix up medicine under Dr Stoney's teaching. Years after, when Mr James finished his teaching, our people would send for him far and wide when they were sick. However, our young sister Evelyn owes her life to Dr Stoney and the fact that he was visiting the Aboriginal reserve that day. I feel too to Mother, sucking out the poisonous blood and spitting it out each time. Father and little Sandy Glass played their part too. The doctor gave my mother some liquid to wash her mouth out. Evelyn today is a very attractive mother of six and grandmother of sixteen grandchildren. She married a Cummeragunja man; he passed away to our great hunting ground. She married again, to a fine fellow who was in the air force in the Second World War.

Such a lot of has happened since those childhood days, since my mother's childhood days, the traditions and customs, before our great tribes were brought together to live and eventually marry. Even our beloved Murray River, Edward River and Murrumbidgee River flow on never to return. Our beloved giant gum trees at Moira Lakes and Barmah Forest whisper gently the tales and stories of our people's hunting and camping grounds. I feel quite often they are telling us there is hope for us all, and the world can be one big joyful tribal ground if we all care for people.

Sometimes an Aborigine from other parts of Australia would invade our little community at Moonahcullah and make his camp in an old-fashioned *mia* amongst us. He would be looked upon with great suspicion by our Edward River and Murray River tribes. We children would be curious, but we were told not to eat anything these strangers gave us. We got used to them after they had been in our territory for twelve months or more. One I shall never forget, he was

Chapter One

Eucalypts and elms at Moonahcullah.

a great big fat old part-Aborigine. He would offer me, a girl aged ten years, lollies. Goodness knows where he got them, probably from the Indian hawkers that used to come to the Aboriginal reserve now and again. With as much dignity as a small girl could muster, I would turn up my little flat nose, and say 'No, I don't want any'. However, I was miserable with disgust when my playmates would tease me about him. I told my mother about him wanting to buy me pretty dresses. My mother was cross and went and spoke with him very firmly. Then we found out he came from a tribe far away, whose custom it was to have child brides. Oh, my goodness, my mother and other older men and women of our Moonahcullah lot soon put him straight about our customs! I eventually lived it down, but I do shudder when I think of those old customs, ugh!

Old Cooka Aggie and Nkuppa Sampson were also another outstanding Aboriginal family of old Moonahcullah, one of the many Aboriginal families who are only shadows and memories of the past. This particular family had ten children, all passed on now, and mostly dying from pneumonia and tuberculosis. I remember the mass killing of our people then—it was unintentional, but nevertheless thoughtless and unkind administration in those days. We were a blot, a big dirty blot on an uncaring sort of administration. I don't blame anyone really … yes, blame is there. Those days we seemed to be just guinea pigs, being experimented on. Governments were trying, I guess. So, what hope did such families like Granny Aggie and grandfather and their families have? Yes, we have descendants who are a little better off, but still bewildered by the rat-race of today. While we spoke different languages, we were all happy together and not divided.

In those days, we were happy in spite of starvation and hardships; we did not know any other life on those Aboriginal settlements. Missionaries were great battlers; living was also pretty tough for them. But one thing I know—our race should never have dwindled. Colour is not the most important issue; people are! When one is called such names as 'half-breed' … while I am not bitter about it, I feel this story of mine may help not only our dark youths of today but white people to see the *real* us! The human feelings of Aborigines, even now, are mostly not understood. Not even by our wonderful white friends! I feel sometimes we are thrown a juicy job, like a meaty bone is thrown to a dog to keep us quiet. This sort of thing is dividing our people, and I feel this is done with devilish purpose. I am happy to say most of our people see it. But greed and ambition get the better of us at times; our living is so hard that we grasp at these. Most times knowing that we are being used! May God help us all.

Granny Aggie and Grandfather Sampson's sons and grandsons were lovable people; they did not make money their god. The Sampson family would share their tea, sugar and flour with us. The boys, when they came home, maybe after shearing or work on outback stations, would think nothing of giving us a bright florin, saying, 'Buy yourself some fruit or something'. Yes, the ghosts of my people are still with me. Granny Aggie and Gramps Sampson's [sons and] daughters' names, as I remember them. Nora: married to Earnest Taylor. Eddie Sampson: got better from a broken leg, caught pneumonia and died on the eve of coming home. Ronald: died of pneumonia. Oliver was married: both he and his wife died at an early age. Bertie Sampson: married a girl whom we all call Aunty Ivy, she is still alive, but Bertie has passed on. Theodore Norman Sydney: he was a great mate of the Clements girls—he died I believe in Swan Hill not so long ago. Helen was a lovely girl. Walter married Granny Ross's daughter. I think he is the only one alive: I saw him about three years ago with grown-up children. He was then seventy-seven, about eighty now if he is still alive.

I can remember seeing old Cooka trying to separate the boys when they got into a scuffle, hitting them with her broom every time their backsides came within reach. She was such a tiny old woman, and old Nkuppa was a bent old fellow. They always spoke together in the language. He was a full-blooded, very silent man. In all the time I knew him, I cannot actually remember hearing him speak to anyone except his wife, even in his own language.

In later years as we were growing up, every evening as the sun was setting, old Cooka Aggie would start to wail and weep for her dead children. As well as the ten who had lived, others died in infancy. We children would gather round the shack in silence and grieve with her. Sometimes the missionaries, Miss McCribben, Miss Bagnell and Miss Brown, now all passed on, would sit there too, just to show their sympathy.

The old lady would rock herself to and fro as she wailed in the language the names of her dead children. Some of us would cry too. Old Nkuppa would sit cross-legged by himself quietly, his head bowed.

Next door to the Sampsons was the family of old Billie Briggs, whose wife was the niece of old Uncle Osley Ingram. Bill Briggs was one of the descendants of Truganini, whose daughter was brought to the mainland from Tasmania by a white man, Harry Briggs, many, many years before. I went to school with this family and we were close friends.

Old Nkuppa Taylor and his family lived next door to the Briggses. The so-called houses were just makeshift places. One of the Taylors married one of the Sampson daughters. Many of the Taylors married neighbourhood Aboriginal people who lived in the settlements of Cummeragunja, Warangesda or Brungle—all from tribes along the Murray and Edward rivers. It is hard to distinguish even part-Aborigines now. It is indeed fortunate that the Aborigines up the top end of Australia are thriving and being cared for by the government. But the main thing is we are people—whether white or dark or mixed—and we are all members of the human race and can contribute to this country and the world in the way God means for us.

Bruce McGuiness's grand aunt, Margaret Nelson, was a very lovely girl whose mother was a most respected resident of Cummeragunja. She was called Granny Maggie. She kept a little shop, the only one on Cummeragunja for years. I can remember the lovely taste of the ice cream and lollies she sold to us for a penny or two. Her goodness and dignity was all that it should be. I can remember one evening after tea, all her family were present and would have to sit and listen to her read the Bible. Bill Onus, her grandson, came in one evening. He was a very down-to-earth man. He saw her reading from the Bible and everyone sitting around. He quietly tried to make his get-away, but Granny Maggie called him back and asked him to please sit down: he did.

Granny Maggie and Grandfather Nelson from Cummeragunja have hundreds of descendants: their fate is well known. Bill and Eric Onus, John, Eric McGuiness and their sister Margaret are a fine lot. Their father died at a great age, a wonderful man, who put us right about Aboriginal history, especially in the Murrumbidgee area. He was also reared at some stage by my old Grandmother Bedgie. Uncle McGuiness always called my father 'his brother'.

Grandfather Noble, another old identity in the Murrumbidgee area, was nicknamed Old Marvellous. He used to say, whether he was pleased, happy or unhappy, 'Ain't that marvellous?' My memory of this lovable old man was his kindness to us children and my mother, of whom he was very fond. He was my Grandmother Bedgie's brother. Some children in those days felt he was a witchdoctor. Mother and we children loved the old man, because he was good, although a bit cunning. He was very generous and shared any food with anyone who didn't have any. He loved his booze, and my father would scold him for it. The old man would go away into a quiet corner and sit down for a while. Then he would say to my mother, 'That boy (meaning my father) him no good. Ain't that marvellous?'

The descendants of those Aborigines, no matter how light-skinned they are now, are of Aboriginal blood and have made the earth richer in this land of Australia which God has given us all. There is plenty of room for everyone. Thank God for this spiritual heritage we have. That keeps me keeping on. I think of all of us as one big tribe now reaching from Moonahcullah, Moulamein, Lake Boga, Swan Hill, Robinvale, Echuca, Barmah, Cummeragunja, Mooroopna, Shepparton. There were no state boundaries before the white man came, and our people roamed far and wide.

I am not a person of perfection, far from it, and I still get cranky when I have all my grandchildren and great-grandchildren around me, not in harmony with each other. But when they have gone home and all is quiet, I long to see them and wonder when they will come again!

Chapter Two

I can remember Lynch Cooper's mother; Lynch won the World Sprint Championship in 1929. His mother died when he was very small. There were six lovely children in that family. An older one went to the First World War and was killed. That was Dan Cooper; many of our lads went. Some came home, others did not. We Aborigines mourned both white and dark soldiers that did not return. Lynch Cooper has passed on now and left an older brother and a sister who was the youngest in the family, a wife, two children and grandchildren. They are a grand family, all of them.

Well, I started to tell of their mother. She and my old aunt would think nothing of peeling off their clothes and tying their clothes and our little tot's clothes on their heads. With we small children clinging to them, they would swim across to the islands in the lakes and other places. I still remember how scared I was holding on to her for dear life. But it was a common occurrence and I learned to love it. I learned to swim at the age of three, along with other small tots.

Food seemed to be plentiful around the Murray River and the lakes, but when the heavy rains came, the lakes and forests would be flooded. After the water went down, you could see the water marks six and eight feet high on the trees in the forest. I visited the lakes and the Barmah Forest not long ago. Some friends took me to the 'back to Cummeragunja' celebrations. It was great fun meeting old schoolmates from both Moonahcullah and round the Edward River, who had also gone to the school at Cummeragunja.

Again, my heart ached when I visited the cemetery. Some of the graves over a hundred years old were just flattened and overgrown. I long for that cemetery to be cared for, the names of those buried put on a monument, and an iron fence built around it.

When I lived in this area, times were hard, and game was hard to get: station owners and squatters put fences across the land, and natural food like kangaroo, emus, and even rabbits were scarce. They were being exterminated because the grass was precious for sheep and cattle. Even fish were hard to get. In the drought years, rivers went dry, swans and wild ducks deliberately avoided flying over or coming anywhere near the Blacks' Camp because the men and even some of the women were good shots with a rifle or double-barrelled shotgun, which was always handy in the house or humpy.

On one occasion, a lone kangaroo was spotted in a clearing in the bush. A couple of dogs were let off the chain, and a gun hastily seized, only to find no cartridges, and the dogs were not the right kind to chase big game. Later, although hungry, we discussed the incident with much merriment.

After rainy seasons, there was much luscious green wild edibles, which we enjoyed with salt. There were young milk thistles, young growth of what white people call dandelions, but we call buckabunge. Beehives were robbed, the precious honey being used in many ways, including sweetening tea, sugar being scarce. Most of our people shared such things as damper and a bit of tea—although sometimes reluctantly. We did not blame each other for that, because it was a miracle if a home had enough food, and sharing was a natural thing to do.

As of old, when our old people were hungry, they would pick up or borrow an old fishing line or make their own rod. I have often seen the old people making their own fishing nets. One day, like many others when we were all feeling the pinch—there was no unemployment help in those days—Mother picked up one of old Aunty's fishing lines. We all armed ourselves with a fishing line and followed Mother down to the Murray River. We looked around for bait, which was easily found after long years of practice, as we used mostly worms. We threw in our lines, holding onto the other end, of course, and sat quietly waiting for nibbles from the fish.

All of a sudden, one of our party noticed the police officer and young constable coming round the bend. Sunday and all, everyone gasped, 'Cunnichman', which is policeman in one Aboriginal language. We all moved our lines and sat on the bank, but Mum kept on fishing. We hissed in fierce whispers, 'Mum, look out', and my cousin, Jack Patten, whispered, 'Aunty, look out, Cunnichman is right on us'.

'Yes, I know', she said.

So, we sat still and waited.

The two police officers came to a halt. The senior officer gave a little cough, but Mum kept her eyes still on her line.

'Good afternoon, Mrs Clements.'

'Good afternoon, Officer,' she replied.

'Do you know you can be fined heavily for fishing; it is closed season.'

Without looking at the police officers she said, 'Yes, I know. But fish has been my people's food all through the ages, and it is mine too, and I am hungry.'

The officers scratched their heads, looked at each other and walked on. We, feeling like cowards, were able to breathe again.

I will never forget my first taste of goanna. One afternoon, we children were all playing together when we noticed one of our tribal Elders dragging a huge goanna by the tail. It was dead, of course. We all crowded around and followed him, everyone asking him questions at once.

'What are you going to do with that, Cooka?' Cooka means Grandfather; all old people were called Cooka or Nkuppa. We kept a good pace away from him, although the goanna was dead. It was so big and long. He got to his mia mia and said, half in the language and half in pidgin English, 'Go get some fire sticks', which we did. He made a big fire and proceeded to cook it. Then we went to town asking him questions, 'What are you doing that for? What did you bring it home for? What are you going to cook it for?' All this time, the old fellow wouldn't answer us. He went on with his business of cooking. Then he told us to get some green suckers—young gum trees about two or three feet high. We watched him with great curiosity as he laid the cooked goanna on the clean green leaves, took the skin off it, broke pieces off it, got some salt, sprinkled it over the white flesh and started to eat it. Some of the young ones, in fact we all, were saying 'Ugh, ugh'. The old man went on eating his portion and enjoying it so much, watching us with his bright eyes. Then he broke off a few more pieces of the white flesh, put them on some green boughs, and said casually in the language, 'Eat'. We hesitated, but we were hungry. Dry bread and tea was not very filling, and old Cooka was enjoying it. The one or two ventured to taste a little bit.

'Oh, oh, it's nice, it's nice'.

Then everyone had a bit. The old fellow looked amused. When some of the children told their parents, they in turn said, 'Ugh, you dirty pang-pang gooks'.

When we told our mother, we thought she would be cross with us as well. But she said with a gay laugh which I will always remember, 'Why, don't be afraid to eat goanna. It is good for you cooked that way, and the fat is used for many things by our people: aches and pains, greasing this and that; it is good especially for your chest when you catch cold'. She went on to say that our people were forgetting all these good foods, and also that my grandmother on my father's side and her Murrumbidgee people went hunting for goanna. The whole part of the goanna was good. We always felt that what Mother told us was right, so eating goanna did not worry us. I cannot remember seeing anymore goanna cooked or eaten.

Chapter Two

I can remember the taste of hot damper pulled out of the ashes, dusted clean with gum leaves and laid on some more clean gum leaves to cool. Aunty had to guard it because we children would be breaking off a piece when she wasn't looking. We drank our tea from a pannikin, a tin mug, without milk. When old Aunty or Mother wasn't looking, we would saturate our tea with precious sugar, which was hard to come by. But that was only occasionally. Wild honey was used when we were lucky to have it. Sometimes we would not have tea or bread. But I am here to tell the tale, thanks to our parents and our Good Spirit, whom we believed without question.

Wild greens, buckabunge, would grow after the rains, luscious and tender, sometimes two or three feet high. In plain English, these were called milk thistles. It is even hard to find in the cities now, to give to canaries. In its wild state in the bush, it is an instant juicy morsel to eat, especially a bunch taken home, washed well and salted. I still love it. Dandelion, when young, before it even shows signs of flowering. The leaves, taken home, washed, soaked in salted water, are delicious to us bush people. We ate yams, the roots of many plants. The cumbungies, growing around natural waterholes or creeks. Their roots, when pulled out, were thick and when cooked in hot ash were very much enjoyed. Pollies, mistletoe growth, contain a lot of little soft seeds. We children loved gathering these by throwing sticks up at the hanging bunches, knocking them down and eating them. It kills the gum trees in the end. However, to this day, we did not have any ill effects.

I don't know where the little bits of sweet-tasting substance, like honey, came from that we found in light bark an inch or two long and in dry gum leaves dropped from the trees in different seasons. We called it 'manna' dropped from heaven, a Bible name. Maybe there is a simple explanation for its appearance at times. To we children, it was like sweets, as good as lollies.

The first time we knew it was in season was when we would go walkabout in the bush, hunting for this and that, especially along the river where the trees are bushy and tall. This sticky stuff like honey in little rolls of bark, or dried gum leaves, would stick to our bare feet. Then it would be on! All the pang-pang gooks or boories would have a marvellous time searching for these God-sent little luscious delicacies. They disappeared as mysteriously as they came, but we accepted it without question.

The much-talked-about witchety grub's home is in the gum trees. Youths, older cousins (nearly everyone was called cousin) would get a tomahawk and a thin piece of hooked wire about six inches and search the trees for this delicious morsel. Then slice a piece out of the tree, about an inch or less across, and then we would insert this piece of hooked wire. Not too big—if it is too big it will mutilate this big juicy wriggly pink and white grub. Although I have not eaten these delicacies since a child, I can say I have not tasted anything to compare with that wood-eating morsel. I often say 'Ugh' when I look back after all these years and say to myself, 'I couldn't come at it now'. But I wonder? I won't eat a lot of things that white people eat and say it's a luxury, such as uncooked oyster and mussels. I've seen oysters picked from the rocks on the seabed and just eaten, 'Ugh'. What do oysters live on anyway?

I do remember sometimes I would see a pregnant mother go to the riverbank, where the water had receded, and the blazing sun had shone on it for days it would be all cracked. That mother seemed to need something in a little square piece of baked earth. I remember we children got to tasting it and liked it too, only in a particular spot. We would grind it between our teeth, yes, and swallow it. I have seen white and dark babies, just beginning to crawl, pick up dirt in their little hands and straight into the mouth. I have not tasted it since a child—from that clean bank of the river. No dirt is so clean as [where] a running river has receded and a hot blazing sun [has cooked] the bank dry. However, I have not had that inclination to eat my country anymore!

Some sort of fungus used to grow in the gum trees. We called it punk, its Aboriginal name. Sometimes it would weigh up to six or eight pounds, all shapes and sizes. When it was dry, we would soak it with kerosene and light it at night. It would blaze for some time, creating warmth and light. If we children suffered with sore eyes, lightly boiled strained gum leaf water would be used to bathe our eyes. If we had dysentery, melted gum from gum trees would be used. If we had a festered sore or a boil—marshmallow leaves or stinging nettles, moistened and hot, applied to the festered parts—as hot as we could stand it.

If we had a cold, our chest and the soles of our feet were rubbed with goanna fat, which was a mighty cure. I believe in it to this day. Of course, when we learned of some white people's cures, we were glad of these too. If we had a cold coming on, Mother or Aunt would give us a teaspoon of sugar with a drop of eucalyptus. If there was no eucalyptus, a very little drop of kerosene. Ugh, an awful taste. It was just as bad as caster oil. To this day, every time I see a narrow blue bottle, I think of caster oil and how we used to be lined up at the Cootamundra Domestic Training Home for our tablespoon of caster oil every so often. Someone would be standing by with a spoon full of sugar to give to each of us to deaden the taste. Until one day I said I would rather have a pinch of salt. I got a tongue banging from the other kids afterwards. They liked sugar. Matron said salt was much cheaper; however, that story comes later.

Old man weed, petibela and pallawah megra in our language, was a powerful medicine. Old man weed is a little shrub that grows very close to the ground and has little green balls. Some people call it 'sneezing grass'. When it is dry you smell it—it does cause you to sneeze. Even when it was growing and beginning to seed, we pang-pang gooks would pick it and sniff it or play a trick on someone who did not know about the effect it had. It made one sneeze one's head off when it went to seed. It was strongly believed as a cure for many illnesses.

We learned from Indian hawkers that stinging nettles made a very fine dish as a vegetable. A weed called fat hen, I do not know its Aboriginal name, is also a nice vegetable dish when boiled. A tablespoon of dripping or butter makes it very tasty (we only used dripping).

I do not remember our tribes in these areas eating snakes—not in my time, or mother's or grandmother's or great grandmother's or further back. Maybe they were scarce or not the kind that was palatable. I have seen films in later years taken of our Aboriginals cooking and eating snakes, which appeared to be rather large specimens. When cooked, the oil of the fat just oozed out of it, so I felt it must be a valuable food. I have a grand-niece (Christina) from another state, a very proud young woman of twenty-two, studying interior decoration and determined to succeed. She informed me that it was a natural food for her people where she came from. I was delighted to hear all about it.

I have not tasted eel. When I came to Melbourne, my friends, who were Victorian Aborigines, went fishing for eel mostly. The first time I saw pieces of eel being cooked, the flesh was sort of jumping about. Ugh! The first glimpse of these eels on the table made me squirm. They looked so much like snakes, cut up into dainty pieces and put into the hot dripping, then to my horror, moving about. Nerves, they told me. Ugh! I squirmed away from it! It was a good while before I would taste eel. That was years ago; now I love it (funny).

The Barmah Forest yielded up its food in abundance in season: crayfish, turtles, wild ducks, swans and their eggs. Those meals came to us without the source being destroyed. I sometimes wonder if the opening of the duck season is managed in an economic way, beneficial to both ducks and people!

I can remember having what white people would call holidays; however, they were useful holidays or walkabout. They did not go walkabout at random; they sought different pastures that were not new to them. They knew that these pastures would be flourishing with fresh growth since they were there last. We Aboriginal children had an instinct for these pastures or bushland. When I was a child, no other tribe would trespass. We were wary of strange Aborigines of other tribes and have, to this day, watched their customs with a little suspicion. Older people do, anyway.

Tales of the witchdoctors and their doings always ended with the good beating bad. Our Aboriginal people were very gentle, simple, dignified people, yes, and lovable. Of what I could remember, they were grateful for anything done and given to them. As with human nature all over the world, they loved you to love and be kind to their pang-pang gooks. The Aboriginal people were not perfect but, on the whole, they were very deep thinking. I remember many times, on hunting trips, being carried on my old aunt's back in a possum rug. Warm and snug, the gentle rhythm rocking me to sleep, little knowing how many hard knocks were being kept from us tiny children. Where passable, flooded areas or rivers had to be crossed. I remember those terrific days watching my old uncle, my aunt and his oldest grandchild (his first wife died), who was little older than myself, come to a river or stretch of water to be crossed. He would get his tomahawk and look for a suitable gum tree, shape a canoe with his tomahawk in the bark and go through the process of getting it off the tree, easing it out with a wedge made of hard wood.

Aunt would make a fire, very hot, so as to dry the sap and moisture out of the bark. While this was gently being done, food would come to light. Freshly made damper, some tea, maybe some fish or river turtle. We loved what you call witchety grubs, but the only ones that we knew were out of the gum tree. Although it is many years since I ate it, I can remember the delicious taste. You can have all your oysters from the sea, or mussels, the French their frogs and what not. Some of the wild food of we Aboriginals was second to none. I saw wild pigs, swans and large animals like emus, kangaroos cooked in a hole in the ground. Especially prepared, they were tender and delicious when cooked.

Before the canoe was dried out in the fire, it would be moulded. Small wedges were cut from each end and stuck through to keep the ends together. Gum from the gum trees was melted down and used to glue the ends. Also, mud was caked in the cracks. Amazing as it seems, I remember as I grew a bit older, some hard-baked earth kept in the canoe, on top of which a fire was lit specially for the purpose of boiling the billy for tea while they were fishing. A few sticks would not only boil the billy can but would have enough coals to grill a couple of nice-sized fish. Of course, the fire would be watched. They knew, through age-old custom, what they were doing.

These walkabouts were a source of wonder and delight to us children. Tiny as we were, we would take part in wading through swamps, chasing bandicoots and young ducks. Old mother duck cunningly leading us away from its young brood, or a swan sticking its neck out; its beak opened angrily, feathers all ruffled, turning on us, as we and our little pet dogs had to turn tail and flee. Possums, when caught for food, would sometimes have a young one, which we would keep and rear as our pet. They were so lovable. When a wild possum was bought home for food, we children refused to eat it. Possums were only used for food as a last resort, in our clan anyway.

But their skins made the most beautiful, warm rugs. Wombat and wallaby skins were used as well. I remember seeing the skins dried out and then treated with something, no doubt an ancient process handed down from generation to generation. This would make them soft and pliable. When a government blanket was available, the skins would be lined with it and would serve as a warm covering against cold air when on walkabout. The women too would put them round their shoulders to keep out the cold.

When a huge gum tree would be cut down for its wood and bark for roofs of bark humpies or huts, we children would be highly delighted. When the tree would have its bark off, we would scrape the lovely moist sap from the tree with whatever we could scrape it with. We would relish it so much our parents scolded us and told us we would get worms in our stomachs. That did not bother us pang-pang gooks! So, our old folks got shovels of earth and sprinkled it all over the tree as we children scraped the last little bit and protested with yells of rage in seeing our lovely sweet sap destroyed.

Our men folk would be engaged to work on sheep stations, especially in seasons of lamb marking. Long tails would be cut off and big bags of nearly fully grown sheep tails would be brought home to the Aboriginal settlement. Some people would say, 'Ugh! Ugh!', but our parents would make us kiddies collect wood, especially bark that would make the most ashes. The woolly tails would be thrown on the hot ashes and left until they cooked. Then they would be raked out. The wool would protect the meat inside from burning. Then when cooled, the wool would be gently pulled off, leaving the cooked meat clean and delicious inside. Some of it would be put in a large vessel with a bit of salt, sometimes pepper, covered with water and simmered for five minutes. When cool, there was a beautiful dish of jellied lambs' tails. That was only in the lamb-marking season.

Chapter Three

I am doing my best to relay stories handed down in my family—handed down for seven generations in a very natural way. As a child I can remember how we clamoured for stories of the olden times, as we called it. Sometimes in the evenings a group of older Aborigines would sit around, the fire light showing up their dear dusky faces and gestures. Their faces wreathed in laughter and smiles telling of funny happenings, which would turn into solemn sadness when telling of sad happenings, I do remember so well. As I see it now, the saddest happening was the take-over of the white race. I remember so well how they discussed and yarned about the boss of this station or that, or the squatters and their families, or small farmers. I can *now* remember with wonder how they were without a feeling of bitterness. They accepted their lot without question.

I did not know how valuable the tales told to we children actually were, such as in the years those great explorers travelled down the Murray River. These tales were handed down from great-grandparents or even great-great-grandparents. My mother's mother, or my great-great-grandparent, relayed the stories to we descendants of how they then watched these white men in boats from behind the shrubs or young bushy gum trees, and ran silently from tree to tree as these white men rowed down the Murray River. They had red handkerchiefs around their necks. My ancestors' feelings of awe were so mixed, we were told; they thought that they were spirits, or some such thing. As they tried to get a good look, they noticed that these handkerchiefs were the colour of blood. The tribe were keeping watch as they always did for other strange tribes, friendly or otherwise. Our old people, my mother's relatives, handed these true stories down to us.

My great-grandmother and grandfather and families got used to the squatters and homesteaders, and the squatters and homesteaders got used to the Aborigines. These white people must have been kindly people; they soon enlisted or trained the women and young men to be of use. I can remember these old station names—the Ulupna Station, the Packawidgee and others—all extinct now like the Aborigines and pioneers of those days. I know the Ulupna roamed far into New South Wales, and around Mooroopna and Shepparton. Only a little while ago, a cutting from the papers of Shepparton was sent to me showing where a very good old estate was being sold, called Ulupna Estate. The names are so familiar to my ears, of old rivers and townships that cropped up in the 1870s or earlier, names that meant something or somebody.

In the early days, there was fear between the tribes. Strange Aborigines would sometimes steal each other's women folk. Human nature was the same in all races, I'm sure. My mother once relayed a tale to we children: how my grandmother went to do the washing or some other type of work about a mile away from the homestead. She was slight and of small build, wiry and fleet of foot. As she walked silently through the dense scrub, she listened and kept her eyes darting here and there. Sometimes she would stand quietly and gaze around, satisfied that no evil spirit or strange blackfellow was around. She knew practically every twig and blade of grass and could see when it had been trodden on by strange blackfellows, white man or animal: tame or wild. She arrived safely at the homestead, finished her work early, and decided not to wait as usual for her father or brother to fetch her. It would be late when she arrived back at the camp. As she crossed the dry creek bed, which hid her from the homestead, she felt some presence about. Of course, she was not alone; possums were chattering in the trees, lizards scrambling under logs, birds twittering to their young, telling them to snuggle down and go to sleep—ever so many harmless wild creatures were about.

As she hastened across this dry creek bed, she sensed a strange presence—and, yes, she glimpsed two or three dark forms between her and the homestead. They realised that they had been seen and called out something; whether it was to her or to each other, she did not wait to see. Like an arrow, she shot up out of that creek bed and ran through the scrub. She heard their running footsteps not far behind. As she passed an old broken down mia mia camp, she cast a quick eye into the shadows behind her and dived under a heap of lumpy bark. She was so terrified, she felt they would hear her gasping for breath. Then she heard them nearby and their spears penetrated the bark where she lay, grazing her body and legs. The Good Spirit must have been with my grandmother because suddenly she heard her name being called by her brothers and father, who had called at the homestead from a different direction, only to find that she had already started for home. It was a narrow escape.

This old couple were from my father's tribe and came from Warangesda. They were a lovable, wise old pair who would often have a walkabout, visiting their many relations. They were many because even if we met Aborigines from far-away places, their totems were the same as ours. Even if their dialect or language was different, they were from the same spirit world. I feel deeply that this explains why we Aborigines are clannish, and in those days did our best to carry on our traditions. We four Clements girls were able to understand four or five dialects and spoke some of it; many of the children did because our old people could only speak the language. Unfortunately, these old languages are dying out and are forgotten by their descendants in parts of New South Wales and Victoria today.

Granny Maggie and her old man would travel miles to come and visit us, to see how we all were getting on. Mostly they caught their food in the bush or asked for food at homesteads as they travelled. I will never forget how poor old Gramps was in disgrace, and I don't know if he ever lived it down.

At one point they were very low in tucker. They were 'meat' hungry and anything living seemed to know they were coming. They had a drink of tea and a piece of damper, their last until some big-hearted squatter or swagman would share theirs. This was not always so, because our old people would rather share their food than cadge from others.

As they were sitting at their campfire eating their last little bit of tucker, they heard a noise up a tree and saw a koala. I am not sure who saw it first, because old Aunt and Uncle argued in telling the story to my mother, when they met up with them. However, old Granny Maggie was telling how they were both hungry, so she made Gramps climb up the tree to get that teddy bear. As I listened, I felt childish horror; we loved koalas, although we had never had one as a pet. They are pretty scarce in our parts, maybe our people used these little animals for their furs as well.

Granny went on to tell us how she bullied old Gramps to climb that tree, and as he got nearer, the koala—the poor little fellow—started to make the most pitiful noise. The old man turned an equally pitiful face to Granny Maggie and said, 'Oh, no Maggie, I can't do it'. Thinking of their empty dillybag and, most importantly, their empty tummies, she screamed at him in the language to go on. Gramps used his tomahawk to cut little steps in the tree, enabling him to climb up. However, just as he got near to the little animal, it would wail. Down on the ground Granny Maggie kept threatening him, 'Get that bear'. But the koala kept making pitiful noises (perhaps it was abusing them) and old Gramps was upset too. He said that he couldn't do it, and the truth was that old Granny couldn't do it either. She made out that she was cross and told him to come down out of the tree and leave the bear. In the language she said, 'Our bellies will be empty still'. I can remember that the old lady told the story as though she was glad that they did not eat that koala!

Aaron Briggs was one of the older sons of Uncle Alex and Aunt Minnie Briggs. Incidentally, he was a brother-in-law of Geraldine and Evelyn, my younger sisters. Aaron Briggs spent practically all of his life in the Barmah Forest, on the Murray River near Echuca. The forest was a traditional camping place handed down from our many tribes. The Moira Lakes and the little islands were great breeding grounds for snakes, birds, pelicans, all species of cranes and the Brolga or Native's Companion, which is the Ulupna tribe's totem. I never tired of watching these beautiful birds, and if you have never seen them dancing, you have missed a treat.

Those great rivers, the Murray, the Murrumbidgee, the Edward, the Darling and the Lachlan and many others, flowed into each other and those flowing waters gave life to the forest. That beautiful forest at Barmah, which we jealously try to keep in the tradition of our Aboriginal tribes of long ago. We Aborigines still believe our people of long ago are adding their murmurings and whisperings to that of the Barmah Forest, conveying messages of hope and encouragement for all people of all races to live and care for each other. We Aborigines must pull together and help the white races to do the same.

Many things happened in the Barmah Forest; it was a great fishing area. When the river flooded, we had to be careful as we rowed through the forest looking for swan eggs, duck eggs and what not. I can remember some of our people getting their living from burning charcoal and in sawmills.

Well, to get back, Uncle Aaron Briggs, like our ancestors, was part of that Barmah Forest. He was very much loved, and I believe valuable help to the forest ranger at Barmah. I think that was the only job he ever had. He lived to a great age and joined his ancestors on the hill not far away at Cummeragunja, where the wattle tree blooms in season and the gums overlook our silent sleeping ones, while the river flows comfortingly by.

Uncle Aaron was a practical joker. He was a happy man. One day he brought home to the mission a huge carpet snake. They are harmless, I am told, but we feared them just the same. I am told that they can be harmful if crossed with a poisonous breed. However, unknown to us all, he had this snake around his neck and would let it crawl into his shirt.

Chapter Three

The Edward River, looking upstream.

He was caressing it fearlessly while everyone kept their distance. But one day someone guessed his secret and noticed the reptile's jaw was tied up. They yelled, 'Oh, look out, Aaron, the stitches are coming undone'. Well, the shirt, the snake and everything was torn off his back and hurled as far as he could throw it. It was the last time he played that joke.

Aaron was wonderfully kind and many times I had a feed of the lovely tasting Murray cod or other fish that he brought home. I often long for a taste of the Murray cod or wild game, especially grilled on the open fire, but it is years [since] I have had it. We long for it when we grow a little older. Yes, I long for a taste of Murray cod, black fish or bream on the coals. I have heard my old people say the same thing. I believe people from the Western District long for eels.

One of the blood-curdling stories we loved to hear was about this old woman who would mysteriously appear at a tribe's camp. It must have been told by many many mothers, many many warriors, many many pang-pang gooks in many languages. Children are called boories and their mothers are called lerroks; women, kring-krings; grandmothers, cookas; and grandpa, nkuppa. Nkuppa can mean any old person, an affectionate term for someone near and dear to you.

The old people would open their tales with a sound that went 'o-o-o-oh', with a rising inflection that immediately commanded our attention.

Well, at this particular Aboriginal village of mia mias, they were a peaceful-living lot. Their children were happy, well-cared-for little boories. One day an old quaint lady ambled into camp. She had big buck teeth, a nose that spread all over her face, and ears so big that they flapped. When the children saw her, they screamed and fled to their mammas. However, she made herself agreeable to the grown-ups and some of the older children, and then left. When she heard the grown-ups speaking about going on a big hunt, as they were running short of food, she begged them to let her mind the children. She made such a fuss of the babies and the little kiddies that some said they would leave their babies and toddlers for her to mind. So, the adults went on their hunting trip, taking the children aged eight and upwards, who love to go hunting, for a day or two.

As soon as the men, women and older children had left, the old woman started to get busy. She told the older children to go and get firewood. While they were away, she dug a shallow pit. When they returned with the firewood, they were encouraged to pile the sticks and wood in the pit, and a big fire was lit. They were all excited when she told them to hold hands and dance around the fire. While they danced, they forgot their fear in the excitement of the game. The old flap-eared woman, or black witch, would clap her hands and sing, 'Knunaga burri-a, knunaga burri-a' till she worked herself up into a pitch of frenzy. Then, with her long stick, she would push the fattest boories into the fire. She did this to two fat little toddlers, and then all the other children took fright, screaming and running away. She called after them in a whining voice, asking them to come back, but they took off into the bush and hid. The old woman cooked the two fat little boories and wrapped them up in leaves and a dillybag and went walkabout to the next tribal camp.

Well then, 'ooooh', all the hunters came back to the camp. Everything was quiet. Mothers started to wail for their little ones. Warriors started searching deeper in the forest till they tracked down the terrified children, too cowed to move for fear of the old hag. But as soon as they saw their own people, they rushed to them, all chattering and trying to tell them what happened. There was much wailing with deep sorrow from the whole camp, especially from the mothers.

At this point, two strange men from a far-off tribe arrived at the camp. They said that they were witchdoctors and that they were searching for a strange flap-eared old woman with big teeth and a nose that spread all over her face. After discovering what had happened, the two men said mysteriously, 'That's her, we tracked her here'. Two of the men from that tribe joined them and they took off after her. They had a hard task finding her because the old mok mok would stand still, so that she looked like a black stump, whenever they came near. However, the good black witchdoctors started to sing and dance their witch dance. The cockatoo, galah and parrots started flying around screeching and making a noise, saying, 'There she is, kill her, kill her'. There for sure was the old woman, just about to enter another cluster of mia mias. When the witchdoctors threw their spears, she yelled, 'I didn't do anything. What are you spearing me for?' The men had the horrible task of chopping her up into wee bits of meat. They threw it all over the place and into the air. Then they called all the children that she had killed to come back, and they did. There was great rejoicing.

That was when possum rugs came into vogue for carrying babies and toddlers on the backs of their mothers when they went hunting. They would not leave their babies or children home with strangers anymore. Ugh!

The Beccers, in the old days, was a cross between humans and animals. They were fleet of foot, meaning that they could run miles in a few seconds—yes, in seconds. Their hearing was very acute, they could hear miles away, and their sense of smell was also very sharp. Their own odour was like the smell of a herd of goats and their bodies were covered in white, grey or brownish hair. But the soles of their feet were very tender, and their eyes, which were small and red, were very weak. (Well, we cannot have everything all the time, can we.)

O-o-o-oh! Once there was a tribal camp with many old-time Aboriginal people. They lived and were happy in their own way. They had a wise old chief and many hunters, and their people were pretty contented. Their children were lean and wiry, and they were taught how to hunt and read age-old blackfellow signs when they were quite small. Many still feel that a curlew, a night bird with a mournful cry, is a messenger of death, especially when they land on a tree above a mia mia, or on top of a mia mia. Of course, there are other signs too, which we would rather not talk about. A lot of these beliefs are forgotten or fast dying out.

O-o-oh-oh-oh! One time two lovely little children with shining black skin, beautiful bright dark eyes, curly black hair and lovely white teeth that showed a lot because they smiled and laughed a lot. Everyone in that tribal camp loved them, they were so pretty. A long long time ago, they were carried around in the possum or kangaroo rug and sometimes in the platypus rug, which was very much coveted.

One day the tribes were called together and told to get ready for a big hunting trip, and to get ready their kangaroo rugs, possum rugs and other makeshifts for carrying younger children. Well, these lovely wee pang-pang gooks were getting too big to be carried but were too small to walk very far. The parents were afraid of Beccers, who had an eye for lovely children. However, the parents of small children took them with them, or climbed the big trees and made platforms and safety cages of strong grass. So, that is what the parents of these two lovely weenie ones did. They were quite safe up in that dear old gum tree. If the children were hungry, they would cry. Sometimes a possum or koala who was not afraid, would grab some pollies (the juicy seed of the mistletoe) and give it to them. Possums and koalas often sneaked around in the mia mias at night, picking up tidbits. Sometimes they would have narrow escapes from dingos, ugh!

When morning light came, the pang-pang gooks were a little restless and were all gazing longingly at the ground. When, who should emerge from the bush, but two Beccers. They peered about the empty camp with their short-sighted eyes and their sharp ears heard the children up in the trees. The Beccers squinted up at the shelters and said in a sweet, whining voice, 'What are you doing up there, my little pang-pang gooks?'

They replied in the language, 'We have to stay up here till our mothers and fathers come home with the hunters, and we will have a lot of nice things to eat: quandongs and cumbungies, fish and kangaroo'.

The Beccers stood scratching their hairy heads and the sides of their legs, thinking, while the children watched them from above. The children whispered to each other, saying, 'We must not go down, our people told us not to'. The Beccers squinted up at the children and kept calling out in their whining voice, 'Come down to Granny, we want to give you something nice. Come on, my love'. They spoke in the language, so one by one they climbed down, all except the beautiful three year olds, who stayed out of reach. These two Beccers squinted at the children in their delight, thinking they had all the ones that they wanted, when a couple of older children called out to the littlies, 'Come down, Nanny Beccers are kind and will hunt for us'. The ugly-looking monsters added their voices, begging them to come down. With the help of the older children, they did come down. But the eyes of the Beccers frightened them, even though their whining voices assured them that they were their mummies. The two little boories said, 'No, you aren't our mummies' and began to cry.

The Beccers heard the hunters coming home, and they swept up the two beautiful children into their long hairy arms saying, 'Come to your mumma'. The children screamed, 'They don't belong to you, you are not their mummy, leave them be'. Anyway, the Beccers were miles away in seconds and the children did not even see which direction they went. So, all the hunters came home to crying children down on the ground instead of up in the trees. There was much wailing and crying from the mothers. The warriors painted their bodies, sat around in circles and had a big talk. Then they worked themselves up from a slow corroboree into a very quick one. They moved along the ground like snakes, then they whirled and they whirled in a wild frenzy of corroboree dancing. Then they lay flat down with their ears to the ground. All was quiet. Slowly the men got up, stood erect, and the chief pointed to four medicine men who were known for their wisdom and great thinking. So, these four medicine men and the chief disappeared into the bush, and the tribe watched and waited. The children slept and night birds gave messages of comfort that these wild tribes seemed to understand.

Meanwhile the medicine men and the head man cunningly circled and tracked these Beccers in their traditional way. Sometimes the Beccers heard them coming and shot quickly to other parts, so the medicine men felt they had to use other tactics. They knew the Beccers loved drinking water, and they had to be down on their stomachs to drink. So, the warriors got to this waterhole before the Beccers reached it. They took a short, cunning way. Then they stood among the shady young suckers and draped themselves all over with green branches to look like extra trees. The Beccers arrived with the two little boories on their backs. Their lovely curly black hair [was] decorated with lots of grubs and little fish, which the Beccers thought beautiful. Before lying down to have a drink of water, the Beccers took their usual look around, to see or hear if anyone was coming. As they squinted round the bushes, the warriors held their breath and stood very still. One Beccer said to the other in a whining voice, 'You drink first, and I'll watch, I feel something is watching us'. The little ones, who were never let off their backs, started to laugh and be jolly. The old Beccer said, 'What are you laughing at?'

They said, 'Nothing Granny, only the funny shadows in the waters'.

So, the old Beccer looked at the water and said, 'I am going to have a drink too, you take too long'. She threw herself down on her tummy. They were both down on their tummies drinking water when the chief and four medicine men speared them in the feet. The Beccers screamed, 'Yak-i, yak-i, my feet, I can't walk, don't take our little boories'.

The warriors took the little ones and washed them clean in a stream, as they smelled like old fish. So, the Beccers learned their lesson and the parents too. Afterwards the parents carried their children in possum rugs until they were big enough to walk.

'Wee-ee-eeoh!' uttered in a descending note is a typical ending of stories from the old people.

To me, the rivers in any country are to be loved and respected. So, it is no great wonder that the Barmah Forest (white people's name) and the Murray River will be a true and living legend until the last Aborigine ceases to exist, and beyond, in the great memory that will never die out. The Barmah Forest and Moira Lakes at the present time are a haven for all kinds of birds, animal life, fish, greens and wild animals in abundance. It is said that snakes won't hurt you unless you hurt them; however, it is best to give them a wide berth—this is true of our Aborigine people. Numerous tribes lived and died around Barmah Forest, buried there among those friendly trees, like sentinels standing guard over our

The Murray River at Cummeragunja, looking across to the Victorian bank.

ancestors' graves. We Aboriginals believe our friends, the trees, murmur their condolences for past happenings and encouragement and hopes for the descendants of the mia mia dwellers. Our lovely, forever murmuring and crooning Murray River gives life to all living things.

Flooding the Barmah Forest in the near future—oh no! Is there no other way? I pray for Barmah Forest not to be destroyed. God only knows we may lose our traditions and our present-day camping grounds, but we still have our loved life-giving Murray River and the Good Spirit, the giver of all life.

These words I love to remember, written by a one-time friend of the Aboriginal people, years ago on an Aboriginal station in Victoria. Barmah is on the Victorian side of the Murray River; we had states or boundaries [in] those days:

'Neath the mia mia's leafy shadows
Where we spent those happy days,
Listening to the old folks' legends,
Of Australia's early days
Gathered round the old camp fire
Underneath the old gum tree
The children with their happy faces
Dancing round in corroboree
Those old days are gone forever,
Like the time our race dies fast
Yet we cling to those old memories
Handed down from out the past.

A happier, hopeful verse has been added by another friend:

Those days are gone forever,
But the future's yet to be,
Where dark and white Australians
Will live in peace and unity.

Chapter Four

I started my first school in Moonahcullah, taught by missionaries, who we loved. I have memories of their selfless giving. They received no salaries. Our schoolhouse was a bough shed; the lovely green limbs loaded with leaves. I used to love the scent of those bushy greens, even when they dried up in the hot sun. We had split fence posts for our seats and used slates and pencils for writing. When our slates got full of scribbles, we would lick the slate clean again. That was short-lived; our missionary teachers got us wet and dry pieces of rag and showed us how to clean our slates and dry them. Scribbling on them was a source of delight, but they cracked easily, and our teacher made us use the broken pieces. We were encouraged by a little reward for the best-kept slate.

I have wonderful memories of these missionaries; nothing was too much trouble for them. They shared their food with us and helped our families when they were ill. Our Aboriginal people also shared whatever game or food they had, and when their time was up to leave the mission, there would be much crying and sorrow. One of the very few who could write would be called on to write to headquarters to ask these missionaries to come back. My mother was often called on to do this. Bless them. It was at their tables that some of us older children learned what mayonnaise was meant for, and other white-cooked food. They asked different youths to a meal when their food supply was plentiful, which wasn't often. We liked their sort of food and the leftovers Mother brought home when she worked at the homestead.

Later, when I was older, I was fascinated by the lovely music the small organ gave forth for church and Sunday school. So, Miss Brown, a missionary teacher, tried to teach me to play. I played it, but by memory or by ear, but bless her, she never knew. One Sunday, we were all in our Sunday best, waiting for Sunday school. While we were waiting, we went and gathered around old Nkuppa Taylor, our favourite teller of olden-time stories. His old full-blood father and uncle were usually sitting near, not saying a word. As old Nkuppa was telling us a story, we forgot the time until we heard our Miss Brown's voice saying,

'Oh, here you are, didn't you hear the bell ringing for Sunday school?' We all jumped up guilty, and then dear old Nkuppa said, half in the language and half in English, 'Do you know we had the Good Spirit a long time before you white people came here. The Good Spirit is everywhere, in the bush he live; him Good Spirit'.

When the missionaries had the time, they would teach us a lot of white people's games. Our parents taught us quite a few and football was not new to us. Our younger Aborigine men were often called upon to make up numbers for football teams around the district. We would not know who to barrack for, because our men would be on opposing teams.

One of the team games the missionaries taught us on our Aboriginal settlement was hockey. We would get an older person to cut young saplings. The roots would be already curved and easy to shape; so we had no worries where hockey sticks were concerned. When the game became faster, our little black forms were more than willing to yell orders, weaving in and out of each other's way, hitting the ball up to the goal. Sometimes the excitement was too much in seeing who won. We would forget the missionaries were there and a few swear words would be used in the heat of the moment. Everyone would gasp, look at the culprit and then at the missionaries. Then we knew our beloved game of hockey would be at an end for that day. Anyway, the missionaries were just as excited to play as any of us, but they would collect all the hockey sticks and balls.

Our parents or older sisters would sew together a rag ball for us. We would play rounders, cricket or football as well. The rag balls were real hard and could hurt if you were struck with them.

Sometimes swearing was done in the language so that the white missionaries couldn't understand. But the missionaries said that bad temper was not good, as the players could not think straight and wouldn't shoot straight or play fair. After the missionaries went home, or visited the older people for a chat, we would try to capture the spirit of the game on our own. But it was not the same as with those lovable schoolteachers, so we would wait till the next day to play again with the young missionaries, who were great fun.

Everyone could play rounders and our parents joined in too. They would bat and the young ones would do the running for them. In a game of cricket, the bats were made of hard board, although really hard wood was scarce.

Football was hilarious. There were not enough boys, so girls made up the numbers. A grown-up would umpire, usually one of our wags with a sense of humour, who would give the girls free kicks and favours. So, halfway through a game, the opposition would give chase to the waggish umpire and give him a rough time. But from what I can remember, it would all end in good humour and fun.

Another game our Aborigine youths loved was pole-jumping. Yes, even in my days it was a favourite. Over high logs, fences, anything. I can remember at eighteen years of age when I worked on the station (of which I will tell the story later), when I would go for the cows or mail, or a walk in the bush, I would pick up a long pole and jump. Much to the amazement of the young daughter, who was about twelve. She would want to do it too, but was too much a lady to master it, I guess. When her young brothers and mates (aged about fifteen and seventeen) came home from college on holidays, they used to try it too. Their uncle, a young man with red hair and a red face, tried to get over that hurdle with the pole. I used to be delighted to beat them all. When I remember flying over those high hurdles, my long skirt like an umbrella, my long black legs and bare feet going over, I can hide my head with embarrassment even now. But it was fun to take part and it was the only fun I had. Oh, plus swimming, especially when the river was flooded. The sheep station was twenty-five miles from the nearest town, although Aborigines lived in Walgett, I only saw one at the station in the three years I was there. The busy times and the shearing shed was miles out, but I worked then in those busy seasons, especially taking delight in keeping the kitchen, board floors and verandah around the house spotless. And at that sheep station, the old Scotch boss would say a simple 'Thank you, Girl, you did a good job looking after us all' after the busy season was over. To me, that was worth all the money in the world.

Another of the games we took delight in was stripping a green switch from a sucker of all its leaves. Down at the river, we would get little bits of mud, roll them into a ball as big as a marble, stick it to the end of the switch and flick. We would have a competition, boys and girls, to see who could throw it the furthest. If we played by the river, you could tell who won when the ball of mud hit the water.

I have had the unique experience of going to three Aboriginal schools. One under the bough shed in Moonahcullah taught by missionary ladies, then in a galvanised shed. When the missionary ladies left Moonahcullah, we had a crippled part-Aboriginal teacher. He was a proud man and would not mix; or let his family mix with the Aboriginal people on the settlement. Human nature what it is, the people did not like him either! They felt they had their pride to uphold too. The wife and children were friendly though. One of the stepdaughters my age would sneak down at night to hear my mother telling stories. Then Mother would see that she got home safely. Mother would want to speak to her parents, but the girl would cry and beg her not to, as she would get into trouble for sneaking out.

Later, at Moonahcullah, Mrs Hill was our teacher, and it was while she was there that we were taken away to the Domestic Training Home at Cootamundra.

Most of my schooling and living was at Cummeragunja reserve. Moonahcullah and Cummeragunja were near to each other, and it was nothing for our people to go and stay for a time, while the children went to school. Some families stayed in one place. In spite of our walkabout and hard times, they were the happiest days of my life. I feel my experiences in childhood, although heartbreaking, were struggles to keep the old standards of decency, which our old Aboriginal people kept long ago. When young Aboriginal men and girls were introduced to the cities and country towns, morals were easily forgotten because of the fascination of white skin and vice versa. There were some genuine ties of marriage, some turned out happy, some did not. But I have found that it is not because of colour that marriages break down. It is the same between two Aboriginal who marry or two whites or other nationalities. It depends on whether they have higher principles to live by. One can, with one's family, go down to the depths of hell and flounder about in degradation, blaming present times or the other fellow. Sometimes I become tinged with hopelessness when I think of the long years of unhappiness and struggles of my people since the white people came. I sometimes think 'How long does generation after generation have to live before we wake up to ourselves'. We allow ourselves to be divided, black and white, one family feeling superior to the other because of colour, possessions or education.

Chapter Five

Mother, as I have already said, worked to help our old aunt and uncle feed and clothe us. When she wasn't working, she spent time at home with us all. She was loved by young and old; nothing was too much for her to do. Like quite a few of our womenfolk, she was a very able midwife. I heard someone say that they would like a penny for every baby she brought into the world. What's more, she showed us how she sterilised everything before she used them: bedclothes, sheets and towels and whatnot were prepared weeks ahead. Once, she was called early in the morning, after a night of bringing these babies into the world. She was having a much-needed rest. In fact, she was so sound asleep, she didn't hear a person knocking urgently. I heard the knocking; so did the mother with her new baby in the bedroom. I was afraid to open my mouth in someone else's home, especially when I heard the lady in the bedroom say, 'Go away, Mrs Clements is asleep and very tired'. When morning came, I told Mother what had happened. She was very upset and hurried around to the home that needed her, only to find that the baby had died. Someone else had not quite known what to do. Mother just burst into tears and the sick mother had to console her, and told her she was not to blame, because of not hearing the knock. The old people told us tales of when a new baby was born in the olden times, ashes were rubbed all over it like talcum powder, because it was naturally sterilised.

There were truly happy times, until food became scarce. Then Mother would be going back to see if her old job was there for her again. Of course, it would be. We would all miss her. We would miss her very much.

She not only cared for the sick people, but would run miles on the other side of the river to find a shallow crossing, at any hour of the night or morning to telephone a doctor for advice; or to beg him to come those twenty-five miles from Deniliquin. Sometimes he would respond, and sometimes the sick person would be taken all those twenty-five miles, sometimes along boggy roads, to the hospital. The road was a bit better on the other side of the river but, at times, the river was too high to cross. Now there is a bridge where white station owners and so forth can get to and fro.

It was nothing for Mother to get up [at] all hours of the night to attend to animals whimpering with the cold, to make them comfortable in a corner on a bag or something. I saw her once help a beautiful proud, fierce-looking eagle that a gun-happy youth had shot, breaking its wing. I don't know how she attended to the wing, but she did. She also kept the fire burning to keep it warm. There was a huge goanna too, wounded with a pea rifle. She taught us a lot about compassion for hurt things, and especially for hurt people.

When I visited Old Morago recently and talked with the Eastman family, who my mother worked for over a period of years, one of the daughters talked to me about her.

'Theresa Clements was a fine woman,' she said. 'There were a lot of us children and Theresa was very good at sewing and would make all our clothes as well as helping Mother in the house. She was clever and she and my mother would exchange sentences in French when they didn't want us to understand. Once, my brother broke his arm and Theresa accompanied my father and brother in the buggy to Deniliquin. There was no room in the hospital, so my brother stayed in the doctor's home while the arm was fixed up. The doctor's wife was so pleased with all that Theresa did, not only for my brother, but in the home helping, that she hoped she might stay.'

When Mother was not working and was at home for a while, she was a delight. She would teach us new games she had seen the white children playing. At night, we would sit around a big fire, and she would read stories to us by the firelight. The adults would sit and enjoy listening too. One of our favourites in those days was *Uncle Tom's Cabin*. Mother would close the book when we started sobbing and crying; the grown-ups too, would have tears running down their cheeks. But, oh my, when she was cross, we made ourselves scarce. While Mother was home, old Aunt would take it easy, smoking her pipe quietly: which only we Aborigines would see, she wouldn't let a white person see. When Mother went back to work, Aunt would quietly take over in her dignified way.

One day my girlfriend, who was the same age as I, and two sisters aged four or thereabouts, went for a walk up to our favourite swimming place, where all the lovely sand was and where our mothers did the washing. We got tired of playing there and I made up my mind and theirs to go exploring the little island bend of the Edward River. It was rather thick with shrubs and high grass. However, before going too far, we climbed onto a big log, which gave us a good clear view all around. We saw some dark forms through the trees—first we felt they were strange blackfellows. We were terrified, and the little ones started to whimper. Our way was cut off. We started to yell and yell at the top of our voices. The good Lord must have heard us. We saw all the women coming around the bend running, old Aunt amongst them. Afterwards, they found the footprints of these strangers; they could have been friendly, but no chance was taken.

Before nightfall, the women made all the children go inside for the evening. They tied up our dogs, the most savage ones tied near the door. Then they got their homemade bush brooms and swept the ground in a circle, leaving no footprints until they got inside the door and fastened it securely. All the Aboriginal women did the same because their Aboriginal menfolk were away at work on neighbouring stations that were too far to travel home at night. The dogs did bark savagely and strained at their chains that night. We lay in our beds too afraid to move and prayed for the morning to arrive quickly. Eventually it did, but the old aunt would not let us go out until she had investigated. She found bare adult footprints.

The next night, we went through the same procedure. There was someone walking round, we could hear him telling the dogs to shut up. We knew his voice, but old Aunt told us to keep quiet. He was a well-known drunk, who we hadn't seen for months. We heard the next day that he had visited nearly every Aboriginal woman's shack or home. He was just as big a menace as the strangers the night before.

When he came to our door, [he] yelled at the dogs to keep quiet, then yelled and knocked and shook the door. Old Aunt put her fingers to her mouth, beckoning us to keep quiet. She quietly went to the door to give it more support in keeping it closed. Then the man's voice came over the top of the door saying, 'I can see you there'.

Oh, we children were terrified, but brave old Aunt continued to hold the door until he went away. This sort of thing happened rarely because the nearest they could get a drink was at Pretty Pine Hotel, nine miles away, and it was twenty-five miles into Deniliquin. Very few white swaggies would wander the main roads those days. Motor cars were still one of the world's wonders, even when I was a child, so was the motorboat. The first one I remember seeing belonged to old Uncle Cooper. Lynch Cooper, the world sprint champion of 1929, was one of his sons. So was Dan Cooper, who was killed in the First World War. Another son, Gillian, proved himself in holding down a responsible job on the railways for many years. His twin sons, I believe, are also in good jobs on the railways. There were also girls in the family, who were responsible citizens and were well thought of.

Years later, after coming home to old Uncle's funeral, everything about his living situation in Barham began to reveal itself and make sense. Old Uncle's tribe spread far and wide and was greatly respected. I can remember he and his old mate Billy Day (whose descendants are numerous all over Australia and, I may say, have proven themselves as great citizens—sportsmen, leading sportswomen, fully fledged nursing sisters and leading missionaries all over Australia; they have married into other tribes as far as Darwin and I have great pride in their womanhood and manliness) worked together with old Uncle Osley Ingram on Old Weeri sheep station, at Caliama and Tulla, and many other smaller homesteads of those days. They were well known for their integrity. Every time they were together, it was delightful to hear them pretend to argue playfully about all sorts of things in the language. All these sheep stations were between Deniliquin and Barham round the Edward, Wakool, Murray and Lachlan rivers. It is such a long time since I was home in that beloved area, the Riverina district—a great flat land of ragged gums and other trees. We kids loved to eat quandongs when they were ripe. The stones inside were as hard as they are to describe. Our people used to make bead necklaces out of them, and jam too when the sugar was available.

As far as I can remember, we travelled these plains, our old Uncle working on these stations; seasonal work such as shearing, lamb marking and crutching, which is done for the sheep's cleanliness and health. Tiny or big, we children took it for granted that a dog had to be whipped for chasing sheep. We got used to seeing kangaroos and emus in the distance, occasionally near. All through our young lives we had pets: young joeys, possums, emus, and birds such as cockatoos, rosellas and wild ducks. We had many, many young bunnies. The cats and dogs loved them too!

It was a never-ending wonder and joy travelling through the bush over vast plains in those days. Camping places were where there was water. If it was warm weather, just a mia mia of fresh green gum branches put on the ground for the comfort of us pang-pang gooks, a blanket spread over it. How I used to love the fresh smell of the gum leaves. Although it was many years ago, it is in my memory just like yesterday.

When the busy seasons were over, the old people would be employed to dig rabbit burrows. My goodness, I do not know how long ago rabbits were imported from overseas to our country Australia;

they sure did make themselves at home! They multiplied so rapidly, they had to be rid of like the kangaroo and emus (blackfellows' food) because these animals ate all the grass needed for the sheep.

One day my uncle and aunt were digging these rabbit burrows or warrens, so many of them, and just as they got to the end of the burrow, they came across an Aboriginal skeleton. They quietly put away their digging tools, after they filled in all the holes they had dug and moved camp. I will never forget the solemness of that occasion, even though I was a very small child. Those burial grounds are very sacred even to this day, and those old people of long ago are still as near and dear to us, as if they were here.

Before old Uncle Osley Ingram died and Billy Day (they also had Aboriginal names), their boss on a station, Mr McRae, passed away. He left in his will that they get no less than a pound per week for the rest of their lives from that station. That was a great lot of money in those days. What a heart that white boss had, or a conscience. God bless him anyway, because the Aboriginal Elders did not have pensions in those days. Our parents, and we children, never did get government aid as others did at different settlements. I do get the pension now and do occasional work stapling newsletters for the Advisory Council for Aboriginal Affairs. We elderly people are grateful for jobs once a month or every six weeks like that. I have been a member since it started and have been nominated twice, running every three years. I have learned a great deal. Other Aboriginal members include Sir Doug Nichols, who has been a member for a long time. Mr Reg Worthy is our Director and Chairman.

Every time my mother had a baby, she would ask Aunty to mind the older ones. They were happy days, even though some were starving days. When our menfolk bought a sheep home from their work, every bit of the animal was used. Meat stews, roasted meat. The men would try to keep the children away while they killed the sheep. We hated seeing it killed, but once it was over, we would be clamouring for the curly gut (sweetbread), heart, liver too, which my mother or aunt would cook in a large camp oven. It was a sort of haricot stew with browned onions, gravy and vegetables, especially potatoes. Every part of the sheep was used except the lights [lungs], which the dogs would fight over. The intestines and the bladder of the sheep would be scrubbed and blown up too. They were our toys.

The marshmallow grass grew higher than us. We would have fights with the long stalks, girls against boys. Then we would run through the stinging nettles with our bare feet and legs covered with lumps, just as a test of endurance and bravery, and for the fun of it.

My sister May, who was taken to the Cootamundra Training Home with me, was a very gentle person. She retained that dignity and gentleness to the end of her life. She was always neat and spotless and had the reputation of looking as though she came out of a bandbox. She married a Cummeragunja man. My other two sisters married two brothers from Cummeragunja.

When she got married, her husband was very sought after as a shearer. May also worked and felt that, between them, they could save and buy a house. She genuinely tried to live for higher standards, and tried to turn a blind eye and ear to what white people thought generally about Aborigines. But she said to me, despairingly, one day, 'A drunken white man in the gutter would be cared for better than a Black man, no matter how well he conducts himself or how well he lived'. I did not know what to say; I felt it was a good bit true. Thinking of my early treatment by white people when I was thirteen years old to nearly seventeen years old; after seventeen, I'd learned a bit and it was a little better. But time heals.

My sister decided to come to Melbourne to work and save money while her husband and son were shearing. They earned good money, because they were good shearers. But, alas, the white people's 'fire-water' (which gave some of my people the courage to mix with white people over the hotel bar) gripped my sister's husband. It broke up my gentle but proud sister's life. She ended it all by taking a deadly poison. She was taken to Echuca hospital and struggled to keep alive, with the help of the wonderful doctors, nurses, and the matron, who was an angel, until her

Theresa Clements and her daughters, Evelyn (top, left), Geraldine (top, right), Margaret (bottom, left) and May (bottom, right).

only son could be traced. I shall never forget how he came tearing home to find he was too late to see her alive. He broke his heart and is now an alcoholic. He is known to be a gentle and respectful fellow, but lost.

My last waking thoughts and prayers as I lie in bed at night is of our coming generations, our sick society caused by selfish ambition and greed. The answer is change to human nature but, believe me, mine is hard to change. I find I tend to over-love my grandchildren and create jealousy amongst them, unintentionally. So, now when they come to see me, I join them all in singing old nursery rhymes and telling stories of old Aboriginal times. After telling Aboriginal stories, I sit and enjoy their company, and they look at me and ask me to tell them about Little Red Riding Hood. I gaze at them; they are more light-skinned than dark, bless them. What does it matter—colour is not the issue; they are beautiful and precious.

One afternoon, my sister May (the one who has now gone to the old camping ground) went rowing into the flooded forest with her two pet dogs. She was looking for duck and swan eggs. She kept her eyes open for snakes, who were also on the lookout for eggs. I remember two men who were fishing near Moira Lakes when a snake made for the boat, no doubt taking it for a log or landing place. I believe one of the men picked up the loaded gun that they had handy for ducks or swans and aimed it at the snake, which was already in the boat. The rocking of the boat spoilt his aim, and he made a big hole in the boat. So, the two men and the snake tipped into the water; all of them frightened. The men swam for the shore and the snake swam in the opposite direction.

However, back to my sister looking for duck eggs. She was rowing leisurely amongst the trees, forgetting that it gets dark quickly in the forest. She got dangerously lost, with water and trees all round, and did not know how to find her way out. Her only companions were the little dogs. She had gathered a few eggs, but she hadn't learned the art of eating them raw. As she sat terrified, listening to the night birds, she imagined all sorts of Aboriginal myths: Bunyips and Beccers, big hairy creatures with big red eyes. She had the sense to keep the boat in the same place and not to move it from that spot. After a while, she started shouting 'coo-ee', but with little hope of being heard. She sat and listened, cuddling her little dogs. All sorts of past happenings ran through her mind, especially the one where she saw a fox stalking her fowls one early evening as they roosted in the limbs of the tree about five feet off the ground. She became fascinated, like the chook, as when the fox first looked up at the tree and then started to walk around it in a circle. To her amazement, the chook came tumbling down, squawking. She was too late to save that chook; but did something to save the rest from such a fate by having her watchdogs handy.

She loved animals and cared for them. She kept her husband's valuable hunting dogs tied up, as he thought a lot of them. One day, however, she felt she would let them off the chain and take them for a walk. They had had enough of being tied up, and she had had enough of them yelping. She decided to take her housedogs too, and a couple of other watchdogs, and a couple of dogs from the homestead. As she walked out to the open field, the dogs yelped for joy and raced here and raced there. A few rabbits raced for their burrows or under logs. Then May spotted a kangaroo in the distance and prayed that the dogs wouldn't see it. But, of course, they got the scent of it and they sneaked as far as they could, ignoring my sister's calls. Then the kangaroo spotted the dogs. In spite of calls and threats, they gave chase. The kangaroo's only hope was a waterhole, a dam we call it, full for the benefit of the stock. The kangaroo, bless it, went into the waterhole, stood his majestic six feet, and turned to face his attackers. My sister said she yelled her head off, trying to stop the dogs from attacking this lovely animal. But they all swam out. The kangaroo was holding his own, but then one of her husband's valuable dogs got brave. He got near the kangaroo, who quickly grabbed the dog by the neck and held it under the water. My sister said she was real sick in the stomach thinking of her husband's wrath, should anything happen to those valuable dogs. So, there was nothing else to do but get a big stick and wade into the water to help the dog get free. She said she could remember for a long time, and even had sleepless nights, thinking of the way that kangaroo dodged its head this way and that, trying to evade the blows that she aimed at him. Those lovely big brown eyes haunted her. She saved the dogs at the expense of the roo; although the dog was half drowned. She walked home with tears streaming down her face and scolding the dogs. She tied them up and gave them a switching.

As she sat in the boat thinking of all these happenings, she heard a faint 'coo-ee'. She answered it until she saw the lantern lights and boats coming through the trees.

Chapter Six

When my father took my mother and we children away from our beloved Moonahcullah, we shed a lot of tears. Leaving our old Aunt and Uncle nearly broke our hearts, but our father said his old mother, our grandmother whom we had never seen, wanted desperately to meet us before she died and that we would see Aunt and Uncle again soon.

We arrived in Gundagai on a show day. Everyone, my father's mother, sisters and a brother and their families, were all in town for the show. I can remember looking to see if I could guess which person was my grandmother, whom I had heard so much about. Imagine our surprise and delight to find a six-foot, full-blooded old lady, her daughters and her friends running to meet us. There were so many greeting us that after hugs and kisses from everyone, we still didn't know who our relations were. There was a big tall, curly-black-haired regal looking lady, who was our grandmother; a full-blooded younger pretty woman with beautiful white teeth, who was so delighted to see us and was trying to hug us children all the time; another sister of my father's who was pretty too, but lighter-skinned; oh, and an uncle who was as light-skinned, the same colour as my father, only Father was six-feet five-inches and Uncle Ernie was much shorter, but we loved him right away. After all the excitement of meeting all our Murrumbidgee relations (the

Wiradjuri) was over, a big surprise awaited us. There were no buggies and horses to take us home.

It was our first experience of walking twelve or thirteen miles, and when we looked from the top of one hill and could see Brungle away in the distance, we thought, 'It isn't very far'. We were thrilled with those beautiful hills all around and the running streams with plentiful trout and other fish. There were rabbits everywhere. We learned to catch them later. We had a happy knack of catching them where they lived, in hollow logs. We would see them squatting in the grass and my sister May would sneak up to the squatting rabbit and she would spring or fall on it.

The beauty of those surrounding hills and the loveliness of the countryside, after living in the flat country around the Riverina district, must have taken our minds off the walk: because the second time I walked from Brungle to Gundagai nearly twelve months later I fainted—a girl of thirteen! Of course, it was nearly uphill all the way, but I don't think I was ever a very good walkabout person.

We loved Brungle (but still loyally loved Moonahcullah in our hearts). Grandmother had a four-roomed, government-built cottage: two bedrooms, kitchen and front room, and she kept it rather nice. She had a nice little garden in the front. One aunt lived across the street; another lived a few doors up the street. Only a few families had four rooms like my grandmother. Some had one room and a kitchen. Some only had one room.

For the first time, we as a family got government rations; the amount determined according to the size of the family. Low and behold, we also got milk. We had to take a billy can to the manager's home, where they dealt out all the rations to us. It was not such a great deal but, for the first time, we children were getting three meals, of some sort, every day. Mother was a housewife trained of necessity and she made such things go far. Fish and rabbits were plentiful, and some fruits were growing wild. There were no rivers near, but there was a lovely spring where we got our water and an abundance of watercress grew in it, which we would gather. Mother showed us how to wash it, bit by bit, because she said leeches sometimes lived amongst the greens. We did not see any, however, and we loved eating it. The water was too brackish for washing, but it was all right for cooking.

I will never forget one school holiday, we were camped down at the Brungle bridge, a few miles from the reserve. It was a lovely place. May and I would go hunting for rabbits. They were plentiful, but we had to be careful. We learned to tell the healthy rabbits from the poor sickly ones. Poisoned jam was used in those days to exterminate them. Men would be given a rather big can of poisoned jam. One person would walk in front, scraping a patch in the ground with a shovel as they walked along, and one carrying the can of poisoned jam would ladle a spoonful onto the freshly scraped earth. The rabbits loved it and would be dead in a few minutes. Needless to say, we children protested and refused to go near anything like that.

During these school holidays, we loved watching the birds in their nests until Mother saw us handling them and loving the birds and stopped us. She told us that the mother bird wouldn't come and feed them if humans were fondling them. A few days later, we visited their nests and found four little birds dead. The mother bird did not feed them because we had held and fondled them. It was a lesson we did not forget.

One fine day, our grandmother and some of the older people, who called her Bedgie, took us climbing up those high hills searching for goanna. Remembering the old nkuppa at Moonahcullah and his goanna, when we first tasted goanna, we proudly told our grandmother all about it. She smiled her wise old smile. But I think all the reptiles must have seen us coming, because we didn't get any. Gran said they sleep in the winter, and it was the beginning of winter. However, we learned how precious the goanna fat was for ailments, such as rubbing the aches and pains in your body, wherever they were. Porcupine [echidna] was something we tasted for the first time at Brungle. It was a tasty dish. We also saw the most beautiful parrots for the first time, the Mountain Lowry. It was delightful to see the pet cockies strutting up and down the street on that little reserve.

Chapter Six

One day we heard our little sister as she came down the street. (Well, it was not much of a street, just two or three houses on each side with gardens in some of them.) We all ran out to see what our little boori was crying for. As she neared the gate, we heard that someone else was following her, crying too. It was old Granny Lizza's pet cocky! Our little sister was outraged when she heard us all laughing. Then she looked around to see who was making fun of her and mocking her. So, little sister wheeled around and chased it two or three yards. As she turned to come back to us, we all yelled, 'look out!'

Cocky, with wings outstretched and screeching, was after her. We held the gate open for her to escape from Cocky. She even forgot what she was crying about. Cocky had given her one big fright!

It was delightful to go into the hills with our father, in his slack time, when he was home between shearing jobs. He would dig a few rabbit burrows, and it was a big joy to bring home baby bunnies. But do you think we could rear those furry little pets? Granny Lizza (my grandmother's half-sister; all the old people at this settlement were related to us some way or other), anyway, she had two lovely big tomcats and a tortoise shell. Well, no matter how safe we would have our little pet bunnies locked up in a strong cage, that tortoise shell cat would find a way of making a meal of them. We gave [up] trying to keep rabbits as pets. I could never see a tortoise shell cat without remembering my childhood days at Brungle Reserve.

A few times when I came home from school, I would see a number of our Aboriginal people sitting around in a circle. My mother would tell us children not to go near this little group, but one day curiosity got the better of me. I found they were not doing anything exciting, only playing cards. They had some money in front of them and some tobacco. They were experts at playing two-up. But the whole time I was there I didn't see any drunkenness; I don't remember seeing that at all.

The First World War was on, and Granny Lizza's son enlisted. He came home on leave, in uniform. I can remember how we children thought he looked swell. Old Granny was that proud of him.

In the school holidays, we loved to go corn picking with my Grandma Bedgie and my step-grandfather. It was delightful. We had never done anything like it before, and many times we filled our little tummies with this lovely sweet corn, which was grown along the riverbanks. Lovely willow trees grew by the riverbanks too. We would help Mother take her washing to the backwaters of the river. The same old thing happened; we children wanted to swim. But I was a bit older then and saw at a glance that these waters were more dangerous. We would have to keep near the banks. We two older ones could swim strongly, but we knew we were no match for these swiftly running waters.

We all got dressed in clothes to swim in: they all had to be washed anyway. May went into the water first, choosing a little bend in the river. We did not dare swim across or go out further where the currents were swirling around, although this little running river was not as wide as the Edward River at Moonahcullah. May and I would not leave the younger sisters on their own in these treacherous waters. Everyone was swimming, except Evelyn. Then we saw her running joyously, as fast as she could, into the water, not realising the danger. May, who was the nearest to her, just had time to grab her dress and hang on. But Evelyn thought it was a game and struggled to get away. She was laughing and yelling with joy while May was struggling to pull her nearer to the calmer waters and the bank. Whether it was over in seconds or minutes, I'll never know. I rushed through the waters towards both of them; because May was slowly being dragged out farther.

Well, this story would not be written if it had not ended well. With May and I both struggling, we got Evelyn to the bank. Evelyn was nine and she could swim, but not in those surging waters—so different to the Edward River where we learned to swim. We scolded our not-so-enthusiastic sister, who now realised what a narrow escape she (and all of us) had. Mother, blissfully unaware of what was happening, was busy washing up on the bank. Our little sister Geraldine (we all had white people's names) tried to tell Mother. But we others laughed at her and turned it into fun, because Mother would have taken a fit and we wouldn't have been allowed to swim anymore, had she realised. Evelyn had learned her lesson and so had we.

Mother and our aunties let their children go out with our grandmother and step-grandfather. He was a very quiet, dignified, youngish old man, with a beard, and he was very kind. However, this school holidays happened to be corn-picking time and Grandfather and Granny Bedgie took us all. These fields of luscious green corn seemed always to be growing on the flats. The one we were helping in was along this little river or backwater. We were given a long, thick skewer-type implement to rip the husks away from the corn, so that the corn could be broken off the stalk. Then we would put the corn into a bag.

It was interesting at first, but our enthusiasm dwindled, then we would sneak away to the fascinating, swift-flowing river. The river had bodyguards of lovely weeping willow trees growing all along, their long beautiful branches thick, and strong arms hanging over the stream. I long to go back to see it again. However, this day I was making headway, picking husks of corn. Our quiet old Wiradjuri grandfather encouraged us in his own way, saying that we learned quickly. The old grandmother would be working hard too, but would finish a little early to go and prepare our meal. As I said, our enthusiasm dwindled, and one day I was breaking corn off, when I discovered it was quiet all around me. I was a little uneasy; I felt that Mother had the unhappy knack of blaming me, the eldest child, if anything happened to my sisters. May always shared her own account of the blame with me. She was a wonderful character and a very venturesome little girl. However, I left the corn picking to go see where they had got to; instinct made me go to the river. I heard yells of excitement and laughter and found all my cousins and sisters standing on the edge of the bank, where the willow branches were trailing in the deepest part of the river. This was not what was amusing these Aboriginal cousins and sisters of mine; it was a little black figure hanging onto the willow branches and swinging high and low in a circle over this rushing river. She was in high glee, having the time of her life.

I didn't have that kind of courage, yet it looked like a lot of fun. I watched, not knowing what to do. Unknown to May, another figure came onto the scene. It was Grandfather. Oh my, I remember his face to this day; it was expressionless. I felt all nervous. Well, when May swung back to the bank, our grandfather caught her and held her. He drew her away from the riverbank. Our Wiradjuri grandfather, who wouldn't hurt a fly and was never known to even scold the children, got a switch and gave her a few good stinging cuts with it. It not only hurt her legs, but the deepest part of her: her heart. She sobbed as she ran into the cornfields. I know how she loved this old man, like all we pang-pang gooks did. Well, we tried to find her for hours, going far into the thick, dense cornfield, but we couldn't. The sun was going down, and we thought of the strange tribes that we were amongst. We had to go to our camp for our supper. I couldn't eat, I was choking with suppressed sobs as it was just on dark now and my little sister and cousins were saying, 'Where's May?' Then the old grandfather quietly got up, not touching his tea, and disappeared into the cornfield. Sitting around the campfire, I remembered the missionaries teaching back at Moonahcullah and wished I was back safe at Moonahcullah or dear old Cummeragunja. I couldn't suppress the sobs and tears anymore, I cried openly and some of the others did too. I prayed and prayed that my sister would be safe.

Then a tall figure emerged out of the dark cornfield and into the glow of the fire, which old Gran Bedgie was keeping alight. Her dear old black face was tear-stained and troubled. She scolded the old fellow in the language, but he took pains to get a plate of food and mug of tea. Then he walked over to my side of the fire; a little behind me, a dark little figure was crouching in the shadows. He made us move over so that May could see to eat the food that he had got her. We did not know how long she had been there. She told me after a long time that she hid when we were looking for her, but kept following as we went back to camp. As the camp was beside the cornfield, she kept near. But when it became dark, she became frightened, not of wild animals, but of Bugenge, the same bogeyman as at Moonahcullah, the Beccer at Cummeragunja, and of wild blackfellows. Our old aunt and uncle at Moonahcullah would say, 'there are no wild blackfellows now, they are all pretty well tame'. I am glad old Aunt does not see them these days: wild white fellows too!

However, as soon as Grandfather came back to camp, his sharp eyes saw the crouching figure at the back of me. Without a word, he got her some food and stroked her curly head, then he got his own tea. We all went to bed huddled together, listening to the night creatures and the wild river that we had learned to love; imaging all sorts of things that Aboriginal folklore had taught us. The river, like us, was not quite tamed.

Holidays over, we were happy to go back to our mother. We told her what a great time we had, but we would never tell her about getting into trouble. We felt that, as she was strict, it would be double trouble.

School again. We were taught by the daughter of the white manager of the reserve. We really did love her. She was very pretty and a good teacher. I did not realise this until a year later when I returned with Mother and my sisters to Moonahcullah and Cummeragunja. I was the oldest pupil in that small school at Brungle Aboriginal Reserve. A boy about eleven or twelve was next, then my sister May, my other sister Evelyn and two or three boys and girls as old or a little older than my youngest sister; about twelve in all went to that school. I can remember a humiliating experience that happened at that school. I was never a straight shot at throwing: playing cricket or rounders or ball of any sort. I could never hit the target. So, you can imagine how dismayed and shocked I was when one day a young lad about eleven years was laughing and teasing me about getting an easy sum wrong. He was such a nice boy that I was not really mad with him. I told him I would hit him with something, but he teased me a little more. To make good my threat, the first thing I could see was a small children's playing block with pictures on it. I was meaning to throw it at the side of him but, as I said, I was a rotten shot. I did, to my horror, hit him fair and square on the head. All of us nearly jumped through the ceiling with the piercing scream he gave.

I would cheerfully let him slap my face to make amends. Peter was our favourite: the teacher and all. I will never forget the horror of that lovely teacher having to give me the cane. I felt I really was an untouchable or a person with the plague. After school, my sisters told my mother, who told me what she thought of such behaviour. I went into our little room, shut the door and wept until I couldn't weep anymore: not for myself, but for Peter, whom I felt was my best mate. We didn't have any brothers.

I said I did not want to go to school anymore, but Mother saw firmly to it that I did. I kept to myself and wouldn't join in any of the games. I felt a deep shame. However, some days passed, and I took a great interest in my lessons, unconsciously trying to make amends to my teacher. I was too ashamed to go near Peter. Peter came to school one day, his usual cheerful self. He had some lollies, which were rare luxuries with us kids. As he gave all the school mates one, I walked outside and sat on the edge of the verandah, pretending to read a schoolbook: still full of disgust and feeling sorry for myself. I didn't mean to hit him. I was so full of my own feelings that I didn't hear footsteps. Then I heard Peter's voice saying, 'I've saved two of the best lollies for you, Margaret'. All I could say was, 'Peter, I didn't mean to hit you'. That little mate said, 'I know, come on inside'. Our wise, pretty teacher smiled at us, and all was forgotten. But I have not forgotten the lesson, or Peter! I believe he has passed on to the Aboriginal hunting ground. Peter will always be in my thoughts, anyway, because he showed me what forgiveness meant.

I might say, the thought that I was the only girl my age on the settlement was troubling me. There weren't any boys around that age either. I questioned my old grandmother as she was having a conversation with my mother about why this was so. She replied that for years the so-called Aborigines Protection Board had a policy or project in taking all the girls that reached the age of twelve or thirteen to the Cootamundra Domestic Training Home for Aboriginal Girls, also neglected girls and boys of that age were also taken. The boys were trained to be stockmen and in other farm work, but they could have learned this on the farms and stations around without being taken from their parents. Our Aboriginal families lived in constant fear of this for many years, especially parents. When we were naughty, at times Mum would say, 'I will get the Cunnichman to take you to the homes if you don't stop being naughty'. Such a threat did not worry us because we knew she was far from meaning it. Mother did not spare the rod and we knew what it was to get a good hard smack on the tail. We knew some sort of discipline was the order of growing up and it was a normal happening for many families.

One day we were allowed to go home early from school. We did not wonder why, we were just happy to be relieved of doing school lessons. But when we got home, the house was very tidy; in fact, all the homes were extra tidy. Rubbish was conspicuous by its absence and we were made to wash and brush up because, for the first time, we were to see a group of Welfare Board members. I can remember how pleased and proud my mother and father were to hear them say what lovely little girls they had, how nicely they were kept and how everything appeared to be so scrupulously clean. Everything was! And what about letting them have the two older girls to train in that beautiful training school at Cootamundra, where they would be well cared for and trained to be domestics and earn a living. They would love being there in the beautiful surroundings and the lovely gardens with fruit trees. My mother and father were listening, but told them that while it sounded alright, they felt that the neglected children with no parents needed to be cared for, not our family, who were happy. My father's younger sister, four years older than I (whom we had never seen), and others from Brungle and elsewhere had been taken. The parents fretted to see the children and the children, in turn, fretted to see home again. Home, no matter what it was, a mia mia or a shack, as long as they were with their beloved dusky-faced bush people and surroundings.

We children were terrified at the thought of being separated from our parents and each other. While we listened with fear in our hearts, our suspicions of these officials grew. I edged near to Father. For the first time, I felt he was someone who really belonged to us and could help Mother protect us. Both he and Mother were both fighting to keep us together as a family. For the first time, I realised why there were no girls or boys of my age on that little Aboriginal settlement. They were taken away to be so-called 'trained' as stockmen and domestics, never to be seen for many years. My Aunty had been taken from my grandmother and, let's face it, many other parents did not see them for many years. Some died away from home, fretting. Home was their people. We all suffered from hunger, sorrow and misery in these institutions. At home, we were all together and free to go walkabout, hunting and doing our own thing. These board members were insistent on having us, but my father said, 'No'. He wanted us at home and could keep us. To end this frightening conversation, Mother said, 'We'll think about it'.

I feel now that help should have been given in a way that taught our people to be self-supporting. Colour was not the issue. Our people accepted white people then, the station owners and homesteaders, as a way and means of existence. We worked for them for food, especially when game became scarce and had to be hunted further afield once the fences were erected. Our proud race was deteriorating and made to feel inferior.

Father had to go back to work, as the shearing season had begun. As I said, he was a first-class shearer. Mother's health was not good. I feel now that she did not feel secure on her own, since the Aboriginal Board members visited. So, when Father sent money home to Brungle to us, Mother packed up and took us all, except Evelyn, who was a great favourite with Grandmother. Mother left her, meaning to get her later. She did not have enough money for one more fare. We travelled from Gundagai to Finley and slept all night under the gum trees. The next morning, a white lady saw us from her home, came over to us and asked my mother to please come over to have a wash, be refreshed and have some breakfast. Mother told her how we were waiting for the mail coach to travel to Deniliquin and on to dear old Moonahcullah. I will always remember that lady in Finley.

We arrived home again to old Aunt and Uncle, who were overjoyed to see us, not minding that they had four more mouths to feed. Little Moonahcullah; no beautiful hills, plentiful rabbits, free milk in the morning or three fairly reasonable meals each day like at Brungle. It was winter in this drab bit of country, where the nearest town was twenty-five miles away over boggy roads, where on winter mornings one couldn't see the green grass for frost. It was our luck to have no water in the buckets and we would have to go down to the river to get a billy of water, our footmarks making all kinds of patterns on that snow-white frost. Some poor kiddies cried with frost-bitten tootsies.

Well! I cannot describe the joy we children felt in being back with old Aunty, Uncle and boys and girls of our own age. We didn't fret for the comforts of Brungle, but we fretted for our sister. Mother comforted us and said that we would see her again soon, that at least, being the most delicate child, she would have plenty of food and that Gran would care for her. We wrote to the old grandmother and sister; we didn't feel so bad when we got some letters back. I didn't realise it would be nine years before I saw her again. I had reached thirteen years of age and was tall for my age. Mother was trying to teach me, without making it obvious, that I was growing up. When I think back and remember the ignorance and pitfalls of that time, the shocked eye-openers I got! One day I was riding my boy-cousin's bike around. It was a thrill after not seeing one for twelve months. Not realising my bare legs were longer (although our dresses were much longer in that age than they are today), I felt free and happy riding that bike around the settlement. Up and down the road, my dress and black hair flying in the wind; until our favourite missionary waved me to stop and talk with her. What she said to me, ever so gently and wisely, made my dusky face grow so hot. I was embarrassed and I hated her at that moment for showing me I wasn't a child anymore and that I must wear coverings underneath. With my black eyes indignant, I pulled up my dress and showed her that I did have pants on. My mother would have whaled into me if I hadn't. But Mother was away, working at her old homestead, Morago, over the river. Old Aunt was fishing up the river and would be home any minute. I felt a sense of guilt and discomfort, but at the same time wondering why, because I had ridden around on that bike many times before.

When Mother would get or make my dresses longer, as befitting for an older girl, I was vaguely miserable and uncomfortable at first. It seemed as though I was being made to stand apart—a little different from my sister May, who was next in age to me. My wise old aunt said little; but dropped wise little remarks.

I remember that our games with the older boys became exciting. Innocent chasing games had a little fear in it, and I didn't know why. It sounds funny, or innocent to say, but I wasn't worldly wise. We were not saints, but the facts of life were not known to we four girls for many years, like many of those who grew up on small settlements and reared with such grand people with Christian principles like my old aunt, uncle and mother, and those old people of long ago at Moonahcullah and Cummeragunja. I cannot remember any suggestive or smutty words spoken—a few swear words, not real bad. But they were thought terrible by we children. We would run home and tell old Aunt and Mother, who would tell us not to repeat such things. I often wonder what made our ancestors tick, their higher moral standards. Not that they were saints, nor was it because they tried to keep sordidness away from we coming generations. They tried to keep that old dignity and strict supervision of our race. When an occasional girl at Moonahcullah was going to be an unmarried mother, the father of that child was rounded up. More times than not, there was a very willing marriage. These wedding feasts, I do remember them as though they were yesterday. There were more Aboriginal women that could cook than not. Everyone would have a hand in making the wedding celebration a joyous occasion.

Mother would have a hand in making the wedding dress, and no one would see it until the bride had it on. The couple would be driven separately the twenty-five miles to Deniliquin. We [would] always choose a good season, not a rainy one, because the marriage would be performed early in the morning, then the twenty-five-mile drive back to Moonahcullah. A shack would be built for them by friendly hands and made to be comfortable. Things would be given—things that could be spared and couldn't be spared—to help them on their way.

The wedding feast would be held in a long green bough shed, freshly made for the occasion. I can still smell the heavenly fresh gum leaves mingling with wildflowers and garden flowers given from kindly squatters and farms around. There were beautiful white starched tablecloths adorning those tables, which were made for the occasion from doors lent from different homes. Short poles were cut from the bush and stuck into the ground to hold those homemade tables up. Then the split posts made forms to sit on, all around the tables. The children had their own little corner nearby to eat. Some mothers with smaller babies would sit with them to keep law and order in their own fashion. Every family on that little Aboriginal reserve would contribute something for the feast and, believe me, in our people's opinion it was second to none.

Granny Maggie Ross, who was hard of hearing, was the most lovable person on Moonahcullah (as far as we children were concerned), she always had a hug and a cuddle and a cookie. My, she could cook! If she saw an unhappy, tear-stained face, she would have a cookie to give. She was Lionel Rose's great-great-grandmother. Lionel Rose is our renowned boxer, whom we are all still proud of. We still hold him, his wife Jenny and their baby in our hearts. Granny Maggie was originally from Victoria. She has many descendants, grand people, making a name for themselves all over Australia.

Well, getting back to weddings on Moonahcullah—Granny Maggie would bring a hamper full of homemade cakes, sandwiches and snow-white (real) tablecloths to add to the other contributions. Fruit would be given, when in season, from orchards around or brought with generous gifts of money scraped up for the occasion. Fish would be cooked in many ways, the old underground method for large game. Many swans, emu or kangaroo were cooked to a luscious tenderness. There would be potatoes and other vegetables and sometimes a sheep would be given by a farmer. Precious rice was sacrificed to throw over the bride and groom, white people's way—when I think of the waste! We children would look on in wonder at the bride in her pretty dress,

Margaret's daughter, Mollie, as a bride.

with lace and pretty ribbon trimmings. How beautiful she looked. I don't think I can even remember how the grooms looked, poor fellows!

After the feast was over, believe it or not, that evening a violin and a concertina would come to light. There was Uncle Jack Ingram, old Uncle's younger brother and old Uncle Billy Edmond, a Victorian from Healesville who married old Uncle's daughter. My, he was wonderful with that instrument. One of the Coopers played the violin and others played gum leaves. The rollicking dance tunes from that little Aboriginal three-man band were something to be remembered. Old Jack Brown and Dinny Myers would do the step dance on one of these old doors laid flat on the ground. After every item, the yells of delight would lift the roof off; if there were any. But all this merriment and jollification took place under the stars, and the highlight would be when a few would do the corroboree. Our people kept the corroboree sacred when white people were present. Sometimes some of the white people from stations and homesteads, the white bosses, would come. After Jack Brown finished his step dance, Mrs Armstrong, the boss's wife from a neighbouring station, got on the door and went for her life doing the step dance. Well, after she had finished, you could hear the Aboriginals' yells of delight and encores for miles around. A white boss's wife dancing at an Aboriginal wedding feast! Oh, those old-time sets and dances; we youth were doing the promenading up and down every chance we got for weeks after. Those Aboriginal musicians were asked to play for white people's socials and dances around occasionally after.

You may think it strange, our Aboriginal people picking up white people's instruments and playing music. Their singing and harmonising was natural; music is one of their inheritances, so is dancing. White youths now play the didgeridoo.

We had ballet dancers in plays and concerts years ago. One of our young Aboriginal women, recently married (her single name was Rosalie Watson, from Queensland) went to America to study. Her husband, Andrew Jackamos, a Victorian Aborigine, is from the same family tree as Maggie Ross and Lionel Rose. I went to school and was a great childhood friend of his grandmother. I knew and loved his old great-grandmother and great-great-grandmother (both sides) at Cummeragunja and Moonahcullah. His mother and father are a great couple, doing great work for the Aboriginal cause. The young Mrs and Mr Jackamos were the first Australian Aboriginal couple to be married in America.

I sometimes wonder if our culture was taught to the white youths as well as our Aboriginal youths today, would it bring white and dark Australians together? I know that up the top end of Australia, the culture and habits of our people are being saved to some extent, although I realise alcohol is taking its toll. I read in the papers today that our young girls of tender age, twelve and thirteen and upwards, are being 'used' in certain mining areas. Then part-Aboriginal babies, who do not have a say in what colour they are, are called 'half-caste'. I do have faith that this will change and that we so-called part-Aborigines will have the right to whatever identity they wish to have; the same as the white people who have the blood of different nationalities too. I am always saying that colour isn't the issue, character is.

Chapter Seven

At Moonahcullah, we had a white manager who filled in as the schoolteacher as well, until his wife and family of two little boys joined him. Then Mrs Hill, the manager's wife, taught us. We Aboriginal children were fascinated with the glorious red hair she had, and my, her temper was a fiery as her hair. I didn't blame her. We were a lively, mischievous lot, but she did not spare the rod. She didn't cane us; she switched our bare feet under the desks. The boys copped it mostly. I felt sorry for her sometimes, because the boys would put their feet up under the desks, where she would have a hard job hitting them. Her face, poor lady, would be as red as her hair. However, we had a great respect for her. But her husband caused many a giggle amongst the children, especially when he tried to learn the language. A couple of the boys were eager to teach him. We older girls were too shy to tell this white manager that the boys were teaching him wrong meanings and fighting words; but he soon found out. One day he was airing these Aborigine words to a group of Aborigine womenfolk. He was so pleased to be able to say something in their language. Then a couple of the younger women giggled. Some turned their backs on him and walked away. The old aunt then asked him who taught him those words. Knowing that he wouldn't say these words if he knew what they meant, she didn't beat around the bush; she told him that he was swearing.

I can remember her saying she could guess who taught him those words. So could we all! The culprit was old Uncle's grandson, a fourth-generation descendant of Truganini, Eric Briggs and also Osley McGee. Both were about twelve years old then and have gone to the happy Dreamtime now. However, as Mr Hill strode away, we knew the boys would be in for a hot time. When the boys heard their parents talking about the incident, they wisely kept out of this white manager's way.

Our youngest sister, Geraldine, had the misfortune to fall on a jagged piece of wooden stump, which created a nasty deep wound, which needed hospital treatment. Old Uncle and Aunt harnessed up the old horse straight away and drove twenty miles into Deniliquin. Little sister was put in hospital, Aunty and Uncle camping on the bank of the Edward River so that they could visit her until she was ready to leave the hospital.

Mother was working at Old Morago homestead and we were in the care of a relation, old Uncle's daughter from his first marriage; who saw that we did not want for anything and that we did not miss school. But no matter how much we loved these relations, we fretted and wondered how our little sister was and wished our uncle and aunt or mother was home—little knowing that it would be the last we would see of our sister, uncle or aunt for many years.

Two, three days, maybe a week went by. May and I were still being cared for by Uncle's daughter. They had seven children then (and a few more, years later), some older than us and about the same age. We were very fond of them and looked upon the McGees as our nearest relatives on Moonahcullah. They always had a lovely flower garden and vegetables growing in season. Unless they had some sort of a makeshift fence around [it], the goats and stray cattle and horses would benefit. They tried so hard to protect this garden with the little scrap they had.

Well, old Aunt and Uncle weren't home yet, although another day had passed. We went to school as usual, and I was thrilled because an

Chapter Seven

Margaret Tucker (at rear) and her sisters (from left to right) May, Geraldine and Evelyn.

older boy and I were the only ones that got a difficult sum right. Mrs Hill praised us, and as I am not too brainy, it really meant a lot to me. Between morning and lunch break, we heard the unmistakable sound of a motor car, a Ford. They were very rare at that particular time, out where we were anyway. While we seethed with curiosity [but] dared not move, one or two ventured to ask if they may leave the room for a few minutes, but they were not allowed. Our schoolmistress was called outside for a minute and she cautioned us not to move until she returned. Like clockwork, everyone (well, not everyone—mostly the boys) got on the desk and took a peep through the window. They relayed to us what was going on outside. A policeman and a young man who was the driver were talking to Mr Hill. Mrs Hill came in for a minute, but she did not take any notice of the boys, whom she had surely seen jumping down from the window.

She was very upset about something. She called Eric Briggs and Osley McGee and spoke to them quietly. They left the school through the back door; I cannot quite remember everything that went on, but then the policeman and Mr Hill came into the school. Our school marm seemed to be in a heated argument with her husband. She was very distressed. After a long discussion, it seemed that Mrs Hill was against what Mr Hill and the policeman wanted.

The children were all standing (we always stood up when visitors came and the police were no exception). My sister May and another girl, an orphan, started to cry. Then quite a few children started to cry. They may have heard the conversation. However, I was puzzled to know what they were crying for, until Mr Hill said that all the children should leave the school except Margaret and May Clements and Myrtle Taylor. Myrtle was an orphan reared by Mrs Maggie Briggs, she was the same age as May, about eleven years old and a very fair skinned, pretty child. Her aunt was Eric Brigg's mother, a descendant of Truganini.

I had forgotten about Brungle and the visit by the gang of men representing the Aboriginal Protection Board. Then it all came to me in a rush! But I did not believe for a moment that my mother would let us go. She would put a stop to us going away! All the children dismissed from school ran home and told their parents about what was happening at school.

I will never forget, when I looked out that schoolroom door, every one of my Moonahcullah mothers, children and babies-in-arms, and a sprinkling of elderly men, standing in groups. The younger ones were away working on homesteads, sheep stations or farms. I started to cry when I saw them all through the schoolroom door. They were not allowed to come in. There were forty or fifty of my people silently or not-so-silently grieving and fighting for us. They did not know what it was all about; but they knew it was something treacherous to our Aboriginal way of living. Not being able to see ahead, we accepted the white person's world to be a superior world. Around that particular part of Australia, I feel we Aborigines were fortunate in having a kindly lot of white station owners or squatters, homesteaders or whatnot. Our Aboriginal villagers did not worry them, of what I can remember.

There they were, all talking at once: some in the language, some in English, some with angry looks, and some with hopelessness, knowing that they wouldn't have the last say. Some had tears running down their cheeks, the children's cries mingling with theirs. Mr Hill demanded that we children leave immediately with the police. The Aboriginal women were very angry.

Mr Hill was in a situation he had never experienced before and he did not take into account that Aboriginal hearts could break with despair and helplessness, the same as any human. Mrs Hill, with tears running down her cheek, made one more valiant attempt to prolong our stay. I did not realise that she had sent our radicals, Eric Briggs and Osley McGee, to race those miles to get my mother. I will never forget her for that. She stood her ground, this red-haired white woman, against her husband, the police and the driver of the car. She said with determination, 'Well, they cannot go without something to eat. It is lunchtime'. We said, 'Oh, no thank you Teacher. We are not hungry'.

'All the same, you children are not going that long journey (first to Deniliquin, then many more miles to Finley, where we would catch the train to Cootamundra) without food,' she insisted.

She went to her house at the side of the school, taking as long as she dared to prepare something for us to eat. Her husband, with his face going purple, looked at his watch every few minutes. At last, she came in carrying a tray with glasses of milk and the kind of food we only got at Christmas time. It was most delicious looking, but we couldn't eat it. We were not hungry. She coaxed us to drink the milk and eat something. However, I remember, Mr Hill could not stand it anymore. He said a lot of time was being wasted and that the police officer and driver wanted to leave. We started to cry again, as did most of our schoolmates. Then, like an angel, our mother and the two boys came through the schoolroom door. Little Myrtle's aunty rushed in with a few other mothers.

Oh, the glad cry of joy. We thought, 'Everything will be alright now. Mum won't let us go'. Little Myrtle cuddled up to her aunty. We had our arms around our mother and refused to let go. She still had her apron on and must have run the whole one-and-a-half miles. She arrived just in time, due to that lovely red-headed teacher. As we grasped our mother and hung on to her, she said with determination, 'They are my children and they are not going away with you'.

The policeman, who was no doubt doing his duty, patted his hand-cuffs, which were in a leather case on his belt. May and I thought it was a revolver.

'Mrs Clements', he said, 'I'll have to use this if you do not let us take these children, ***now***.'

Thinking the policeman would shoot Mother because she was making such a fuss, we screamed, 'Oh, we'll go with him, Mum, we'll go'. In my heart, I cannot forget any detail. It stands out as though it were yesterday. I could not ever see kittens taken from their mother and drowned without remembering that scene, although it is just on sixty years ago.

However, the policeman must have had a heart, because he allowed my mother to come in the car with us three girls as far as Deniliquin. She had no money and only the clothes she had on. Then the policeman sprung another big shock.

He said we had to go to Deniliquin hospital to pick up Geraldine, who was to be taken as well. The horror on my mother's face and her heartbroken cry; I try to wipe it from my memory. All she could say was, 'Oh no, not my baby. Please, let me have her. I will look after her'.

As that policeman walked up the hospital path to get my little sister, May and I sobbed quietly. Mother got out of the car and stood wailing with a hopeless look. Her tears had run dry, I guess. I thought to myself, I will gladly go, if they will only leave our little sister Geraldine with my mother.

'Mrs Clements, you can have your little girl. She left the hospital with her aunt and uncle early this morning,' said the policeman.

Mother simply took the policeman's hand and kissed it, saying, 'Thank you, thank you'.

Then we were taken around to the police station, where the policeman no doubt had to report. Mother followed him, thinking she could beg once more for us, only to rush out when she heard the car start up. My last memory of her for many years was her waving pathetically, as we waved back. May and I were crying, 'Goodbye Mum, we'll be all right, don't cry—pray, Mum'. But we were too far away for her to hear us.

I heard years later, how after watching us go out of her life, she wandered away from the police station and walked three miles along the road leading out of town to Moonahcullah. She was worn out, with no food, no money, and with her apron still on. She wandered off the road a little, so exhausted that she lay down to rest on some long grass under a tree. That is where old Uncle and Aunty found her the next day. When they had arrived back at Moonahcullah with little sister, our people told them the whole story. They were immediately offered the loan of a fresh horse to go back to find Mother. They found her, still crying and moaning. They would not have found her, only they

Mrs Tucker (arrowed) with her mother and three sisters.

Memories hold a fragile history

By LOUISE CARBINES

 the front of her autobiogra-hy, Mrs Margaret Tucker wrote arefully: "Thank you for your isit. Come any time. You are elcome."

She held out the book, frown-g at the shaky letters. Eyes idening, she leant closer. "I am etting old," she whispered, miling. "Our people are scat-ered now, and some of the young nes have blonde hair."

Balancing on her cane, she wered herself on to the couch. he pinned back the hair that ad strayed into her eyes. It is lmost as long as it was when she as a girl.

Mrs Tucker is 80. She was born Moonahcullia in northern Vic-ria. She lives in a Housing ommission flat in North Mel-ourne. Like thousands of Abori-nal girls, she was taken from er parents by the Aboriginal rotection Board and put into omestic service.

"It was just like taking little uppies away to drown them, d watching the mother get up follow them," she said. "That's w it comes to me now. I don't ow whether it's still going on.

"When the inspector came to hool to take us away, another original woman said to one of e boys: 'Run like mad to get eir mother'.

"My mother came running, ll with her apron on. She put r arms around us, and we held to her tightly. She said: hey're not neglected. See, ey're well dressed'. The last saw of her, she was walking and down in front of the lice station, crying and wring-g her hands."

The Aboriginal Protection Act 1909 allowed the Government take "neglected" children om their parents. The board's ficers usually pronounced the ildren neglected if their rents had no fixed plac... ode.

The stories of Mrs Tucker's generation are unfamiliar to many whites. Aborigines are working hard to collect these stories, knowing that Aboriginal history is as fragile as the old people who carry it with them. Today, the Aborigines Advancement League is holding a seminar on Aboriginal culture and ways of retaining it.

Mrs Tucker was 13 when she was sent to the Cootamundra Domestic Training Home for Aboriginal girls. Her sister, May, was also taken to the centre. "May fretted so. I don't think that she would mind me saying this, but she was very unhappy about what happened to her people. She took her own life when she was only a young woman.

"Going to those homes was the done thing. It was taken for granted. It was a mistaken idea of helping Aboriginal girls. I don't hold anything against the people who did it. At the time, it broke our hearts.

"When our new employers sent for us, we had been trained only for a few weeks. But they forgot that we were brought up in little humpies. We learned to wash up, and to clean their clothes, but sometimes we made mistakes.

"Once, the dye in my mistress's stockings colored the washing. I nearly lost my legs over it. I've still got marks on my legs from the beating. The mistress cried and yelled. I thought, I'm the one who has got the wounds. What's she fainting for?

"Being with white people, I copied their way of speaking. I spoke the best I could.

"Later, I married a white man. I knew that it was taboo. My husband thought the world of me. He was jealous, too. My mother-in-law fainted when she heard that her son was going to marry an Aboriginal girl. But on her ...athbed, she said: 'You're more a lady than my son's a gentleman'".

Mrs Tucker belongs to a small group of Aboriginals who have written the stories of their childhood. Researchers are concerned that so little of the oral history of Victorian elders had been reco...ed.

An Aboriginal research student at La Trobe University, Mr Wayne Atkinson, said yesterday that the need to take down the oral history of Aborigines was becoming extremely urgent.

"We have to salvage quickly so much information which ...ould be lost," Mr Atkinson sa...

"It's impo... our own peo...

"Ninety-... Aboriginal ... written by ... are hoping t... ria's 150th a... tions, we co... finance to ...

Mrs Margaret Tucker: "It was just like taking puppies away to drown them, and ... mother get up to follow them."

An article in *The Age*, in 1984, about the publication of Margaret's book.

heard this moaning and thought it was an animal in pain. Being fond of animals, old Uncle stopped the horse and got out of the buggy to investigate. Aunty heard him talking in the language and protesting about something. She got down from the buggy and hurried to old Uncle's side. They found our mother half demented and ill. They gave her water and tried to feed her, but she couldn't eat. She was ill and wasn't interested in anything for weeks. She wouldn't let Geraldine out of her sight. She slowly got better, but I believe for months after, at the first sight of a policeman's white helmet coming around the bend of the river, she would grab her little girl and run to escape into the bush. Almost all the Aboriginal people who had children on the settlement did likewise.

When these happenings reached the ears of the squatters and the farmers, they got together and protested. I believe they got an assurance that Mother and her little girl would be left alone. Mother was ill for a long time, but with love and care from all her Aboriginal people on the settlement, especially faithful old Uncle and Aunt and, with courage, she was her old self again: up and doing. I often wonder how many other Aboriginal children were taken like this and if this sort of happening still goes on.

It was not long before our Aboriginal people started moving to other places, their ancestral grounds such as around Kerang, Wakool, Barham, Moulamein, Balranald and Swan Hill and other places. Some went to the settlements at Cummeragunja and Warangesda—all over the place where the Murray River, the Edward River and the Murrumbidgee River flow.

The same thing happened at Cummeragunja, where I had most of my education under Mr James's tuition. Young girls were taken by force in a cruel manner, especially when our Aboriginal fathers and men were away working. At Cummeragunja, the girls, aged thirteen or fourteen, swam the Murray River to escape to the Victorian side. I believe a policeman resigned from the force saying if it was a policeman's job to tear crying children from heartbroken mothers, he did not want the job.

Some girls did not ever return. At Cootamundra Domestic Training Home, little Coralie Allen was isolated from the rest of us because she had TB, an illness that killed a lot of our people both on Moonahcullah and Cummeragunja. She used to beg to have her bed near the other girls; she was afraid on her own. The girls would hear her whimpering pitifully, 'Please, Matron, I'll be a good girl. I won't be naughty'. Matron Rutter, whom I had great respect for, would talk with her and tell her she was a sick little girl and a good girl, not a naughty one. She went on to explain that she was kept away from us because we would disturb her and worry her. Then we would hear Matron telling her a couple of stories. I don't remember if she was there very long, but she was one of the girls who didn't see her people again.

Chapter Eight

When May, Myrtle and I arrived at Cootamundra railway station in the care of Mr Hill, who should we see standing on the platform—our father and Uncle Ernie Clements. May and I ran to them. We thought, 'We will be all right this time'. I will never know how [they] knew we would be arriving by that train. But our joy was short-lived. A policeman was there to meet us also, and a horse-drawn cab.

The Cootamundra Domestic Training Home for Aboriginal Girls was, I believe, a hospital before it became the Home. It had one long, wide room in the centre with rows of beds on each side, a row of beds end-to-end, up the middle of the room. It was embarrassing the first night. I didn't have a nightgown or any clothes to speak of, as we were not allowed to go home to pack our things before we left. There was another long room called the dormitory, with about half a dozen beds, and another with so many beds in it. It is so long ago I can't quite remember the layout. I do remember Matron and the assistant matron had quarters leading into the end of the dormitory. However, we fitted into this family of girls, about thirty-odd, coming and going all the time. They gave us the lowdown on what was what. The girls told us that Matron was a good sort—her bark was worse than her bite. But the assistant matron was very bad tempered. She was a tall, well-built

Cootamundra Domestic Training Home for Aboriginal Girls, now Bimbadeen College.

woman. I thought that she was rather pretty. Her name was Miss Wood. She had a little boy whom we all loved. She did the meals and taught two girls the cooking: two different girls each week. And, believe me, they were too scared of her to concentrate and were very much relieved when their week was up. She only showed you once and expected you to remember.

The school was in the grounds. We three all attended school the first day, but I was kept from school the next day on the grounds that I was too big. I was only thirteen years old, but the officials called me 'the overgrown fourteen year old'. I protested and said that my mother ought to know my age. However, that was the last time I went to school. I think I was thirteen years and four months.

The first morning, we couldn't eat the porridge that we were given for breakfast. You might think this strange, seeing that food was not plentiful on the settlement, although our menfolk were mostly away working as stockmen, drovers, shearers and lamb marking in season. We couldn't eat the porridge that was given to us. No doubt it was wholesome, but sugar was rationed, and I can remember it was a funny brown colour. However, the other girls begged us to give it to them, and as I watched them finish our porridge for us, they explained that no-one was allowed a second helping of anything. They also told us that we would be glad to eat what was put before us in a day or so. And sure enough, we not only ate what was put before us, but we marched into the dining hall and sang grace. The girls would sometimes barter with each other for a bigger share, in exchange for something precious. Many keepsakes from home exchanged hands because of the pangs of hunger. Sometimes a girl would greedily pinch the food off the plate next to her. Then there would be tears or a quiet brawl so Miss Wood or Matron would not see. When I look back now, I feel sure that it was Miss Wood who was in charge of the food and cooking.

When the Protection Board visited the Home, which they did at various times, some of them would speak with the girls and ask them how they were getting on. One or two spoke up and said we did not get enough to eat. At that, the men would say that it couldn't be true because the food bill for the Home was enormous.

I wasn't there very long before I was chosen, along with Beatrice Bugg, a girl of fourteen, to help Miss Wood in the kitchen that week. For three days or so, we managed to get by. Then she tried to teach us how to cook and ice a cake. Well, try to imagine Aborigine girls coming from camp life; no stoves, only open fires and a three-legged camp oven that was used to cook everything from a roast to a dish called sea pie. This pie had a lovely crust; my mother and aunt used to be experts at it. Also, sweets such as rice or sago pudding and the very rare plum pudding boiled in a kerosene tin that had been washed out until it was free from the taste and smell of the kerosene. The damper was cooked in the ashes and dusted clean with leaves from the gum tree suckers. It would be as clean as the scones cooked [in] the oven. You can regulate the heat to your liking in any kind of stove, but you had to have a technique and know how to regulate cooking in an open fire.

Of course, it was very rarely that people in these settlements had two meals a day, other than a slice of damper, with or without dripping (Ugh!), treacle or, very rarely, golden syrup. Golden syrup was liked, but it wasn't plentiful enough to become disliked! If we were lucky enough to have a rabbit or a little piece of meat, it would be put into the biggest pot we had, with an onion or potato if we had them. Or we would go around the settlement cadging for one. It was never hard to get salt. Thickened with flour, oh, that soup and spoonful of meat was the most delicious concoction you ever tasted. We children got used to not knowing where the next meal was coming from. However, I am here to tell the tale and to ask why we were expected to understand white people's disciplined cooking and meals, we children of the bush, within a week? Then we got belted up by the assistant matron the week we did our turn in the kitchen.

I often wonder where Beatrice Bugg is now. She was a very nice girl. I can remember that day, I got smacked for not remembering things like vanilla essence: essence of this, essence of that. It was the first time we were ever introduced to such things as the plentiful array of tins and canisters and cupboards packed with things in that kitchen. I remember my mate Beatrice' bleeding lips and bruised cheeks. She was slightly bigger than me, and I cowered in the corner of the kitchen while Miss Wood wielded a good-sized piece of firewood. Her face was red and awful looking; poor Beatrice, I will never forget it, or what it led to.

Matron was upset when she came into the kitchen. The girls were standing around, but far enough away not to be involved. They were terrified, some were crying. Matron, however, broke it up with difficulty. Miss Wood was like a mad person. As soon as we could slip through the kitchen door, I remember clutching Beatrice's arm, still crying, and saying, 'Come on, mate, let's find a place to hide where Miss Wood won't find us'.

Matron's way of punishing naughty girls was different, more lenient. Once, she was conducting Sunday school. We were all assembled in the hall of the dining room. Two or three of the girls were restless and playing up. However, she called them out and stood them with their faces turned to the wall. Matron was talking to us all, but we could not concentrate on the Sunday school story because [of] one of the girls behind Matron (Myra), who was supposed to have her face to the wall. Myra created merriment by peeping around from the wall and grimacing. No doubt she was feeling embarrassed being punished in front of the room full of her mates. But she was getting a little encouragement with her fun-making because the girls giggled. She started to lightly finger Matron's long white veil. However, Matron chanced to look around at the moment the girl was holding the veil, and the veil (I suppose pinned lightly onto Matron's hair) was pulled off Matron's head.

Matron looked horrified and the girl looked terrified! Matron just got hold of that girl, bent her over her knee, lifted her dress and belted her with her bare hand. I do not know which was the most sore: Matron's hand or the girl's bottom. Although the girl was naughty, we were all sorry for her humiliation. There are a lot of Myras in the world—full of mischief. But I know there is an answer to all frustration and bitterness, which I didn't know then.

We just accepted these happenings, although my sister May and Myrtle and I would get homesick and we would go to a quiet corner of the building to talk about home; our mother, aunties, sisters, brothers or cousins, and wonder when we would see them again. Then we would have a good old cry, getting the homesickness out of our systems for a while anyway. There were many lonely little girls there without a sister or cousin, so the bigger girls would unofficially adopt one as a sister. I can remember now how pathetically these little ones would love to be included or to belong. We were all accepting that ahead was the unknown—just as well we did not know.

The night after Miss Wood's attack on us, we older girls gathered together and had what you might call a consultation. The outcome was that nine of us decided to run away. The thought of going into that kitchen again with Miss Wood, this big woman who belted us up, was too much. Well, we were not brave, and our courage was petering out, so we did not let the grass grow under our feet. We crept in to say goodbye to our sisters and friends when everyone was asleep, and things were quiet. Well, my sister May, Myrtle and little Lillian Foster, whom we had chosen to take under our wing, all wept.

We nine then all threw our boots out of the high window and grabbed a blanket each. It was June or July, I think. I know it was winter! Then we collected our boots. We had thick, unsightly homemade woollen socks, printed blouses and long ugly grey winceyette skirts on. As we felt for our boots, someone either did not throw their boots out or couldn't find a pair in the dark. However, I can remember squeezing on a pair, which I realised weren't mine. Anyway, someone else had mine, and I distinctly remember throwing my boots out the window. Mary Hickey said to me, 'Someone has my boots. I think you have them, Margaret'. Although the boots were hurting me like the dickens, I said, 'No, they are mine'. However, after limping a half mile or so, I couldn't stand the pain any longer and became grudgingly honest. I said, 'I think they must be yours, Mary. Someone else must have mine on, or they must be back under the window at the Home'.

Chapter Eight

The dormitory at Cootamundra.

Then someone said that a strip of the end of the blankets would make a covering for my feet. Anything was better than nothing. Well, I cannot describe what my feet looked like. It was night-time, but they looked hilarious when the daylight came! We went pretty far, for us, that night. An older girl called Diddi, I think her real name was Ella Murray, was sort of the leader of the group. However, some of us were getting tired, thirsty and hungry. We drew lots to see who would cadge some tucker from the next farmhouse. We didn't know what time it was, but we came to a cottage or farmhouse. It had a dim light in it and the dogs began to bark. The three girls chosen stuffed some of their belongings down their blouses, I remember their chests looked like pigeons. When the three girls went to this house to cadge something to eat, we others waited expectantly. As we heard them coming back, Georgina Barlow, the same age as I and very pretty, was highly indignant and calling the man all sorts of names. However, he said that his wife had gone to hospital to have their baby. The girls told him story of how they were short of food and were travelling.

Anyway, seeing Georgina Barlow, only thirteen years, with her blouse all puffed out where she had some of her clothes stuffed, his curiosity got the better of him. He rubbed his hands down the front of her blouse, so she bolted back to us, the other two were close on her heels. Some of the girls giggled at her and said, 'No wonder'. But that was the end of going to any more farms or houses. We all had a thirst, and I had a raging one. It must have been one or two o'clock in the morning. We could see this waterhole. Probably the sheep and horses all drank at it. So, to add to that we Aboriginal girls laid on our stomachs and drank that water. Ugh! Then Diddi, our leader, said, 'Don't drink anymore'. But I was thirsty, and I meant to have my fill. So, I greedily gulped some more. Diddi said, 'There is a tree, we'll spread our blankets and rest for a little while; but we must keep on moving'. We all snuggled together and I was soon asleep. We were awoken by snorting and huge feet of draught horses tramping around us. I thought, 'Oh, no' but 'Oh, yes', huge draught horses! I don't know how many, but they probably resented us camping on their ground and they really were making a fuss. Diddi yelled to us to get up quick. We grabbed our blankets and belongings and made for the fence, the horses still indignant for our intrusion on their sacred ground.

I was scared. I remembered the time when Mother and we four little daughters travelled from Moonahcullah by horse and buggy to Deniliquin, where we got the old train to Cummeragunja. We got out at a little railway siding called Moira siding, and we had to walk across a paddock to Moira station. Just as we got to the centre of this paddock, Mother noticed some horses. She said to us little girls, 'Oh, keep walking, there is a stallion and he has his head up looking at us. Keep walking, don't be afraid'. But we were afraid, because this stallion started to walk towards us. We were about one hundred yards from the fence when the stallion started to trot. Mother cried to us to run and we did! We looked to see if Mother was running, but she was terrified for us and kept the stallion's interest while we scrambled and fell through the fence. We yelled and begged for Mother to run. She was so near the fence when the horse stopped being curious and started to trot towards Mother. We cried and yelled, 'Come on, Mum, run, oh run quick!' She ran, and with all our might we stretched the fencing wire up so that she could get through quickly. She just rolled through and lay there until she got her breath. Then she screamed at us to get away from the fence. It's funny, I love horses now, but deep down I am afraid of them.

Diddi said that it was best to keep walking, and then (oh my, why did everything happen to me) I started to get dreadful pains that made me cry. I still had my blanket slippers, or flippers, for they were coming undone and flapping on the ground as I walked. I couldn't bear it. I thought to myself, 'It is my fault, I would be greedy and drink and drink that water, which must have been full of tadpoles and whatnot'. Two of our mates got each side of me and helped me along. Diddi said that the pain might go away, which it did.

I don't know how long we were walking in the direction of Muttama, where Uncle Ernie Clements worked. Muttama was twelve miles from Cootamundra, and we reached this place just before sunrise.

We followed the railway line and, although tired and hungry, we liked the countryside. It was lambing season and these lovely little creatures were everywhere with their mothers. Then we were all very concerned for one little lamb, which was born in the mouth of a rabbit burrow. It tried every way to get its hindquarters out of that burrow, but it was stuck, and the mother was bleating piteously. Then Diddi had a brainwave and said we could kill it, make a fire and grill it. As much as we were hungry, we were horrified at the suggestion. We tried to free the poor thing, but the ground was so hard that we couldn't even dig with sharp sticks. Then Diddi said we could let someone know; however, there was no need because a man on horseback came riding towards us.

We told him about the wee lamb, but he didn't seem to worry about the lamb. He was more interested in us and asked us if we came from that school on the side of the hill in Cootamundra. The girls said, 'Oh no, we are just travelling'. Anyway, he told us that word had got to all the farms and homesteads, that nine girls had run away. He asked us to follow him back to his home, where a nice breakfast would be waiting for us. That did it; we were hungry and tired. I was embarrassed with my blanketed feet and tried to hide behind the girls, but it was difficult. We got to his house and, sure enough, his good wife had hot scones, plenty of jam and butter and lovely milky tea. I felt that anything was better than running away. I had had it. My feet were sore—I was never good at walkabout.

Judging by the looks on the girls' faces, we were ready to go back and face the music. So, the gentleman and his wife got we nine girls to a little railway station by car and sulky. We reached Muttama railway station and caught the train back to Cootamundra. The fellows at the railway station had a sense of humour. They called out, 'Welcome to the runaways', as we got out of the train. We were lined up, and there was a policeman and Miss Wood waiting for us. We landed back at the Home, and as we lined up, I tried to hide my feet again, but it was no use. Miss Wood pointed me out and said, 'You ought to be ashamed of yourself, Margaret'. My word, I was. We were all locked up in different parts of the

Home. Beatrice and I had a bathroom each, with a leaden-looking floor and one blanket. It was a freezing and frightening experience because we all believed in ghosts. It was the first time I, as a girl of thirteen, had experienced a touch of rheumatism. We were given dry bread and water as punishment.

A month or so passed and we settled down again and tried to accept our lot. One day Matron Rutter sent for Beatrice and me. We found her sitting in the sewing room with piles of material, brown and some other colours. Then we were measured and fitted. I thought, 'Oh, we are going to have some new clothes'. Anything was better than the old winceyette skirts and those print blouses. When we told the girls, who were pretty curious and wondering why we were summonsed into Matron's quarters, they said, 'Oh, you lucky things, you are going away to service'. May and Myrtle started to cry. I felt not quite so happy about it—we were to be parted again. I did not realise that my sister May was very delicate. She fretted quite a bit for home. I was so glad that she and Myrtle would still be together. But I didn't know that Myrtle would be sent to a Home for white girls, because she was very fair and pretty. She was a shy girl, but she had a lovely singing voice and we would coax her to sing when we were together in a quiet spot.

Well, the outcome was that Beatrice and I were sent to our situations. Oh, the excitement of just the two of us travelling in the train on our own to Sydney! I was thirteen years old, the year was 1919: 55 years ago. As I sit and think, my thoughts run back to saying goodbye to my sister May and Myrtle. I did not realise these partings from our loved ones at Moonahcullah, running away from the Home, and then parting to go to my situation in Sydney all took a toll on May. I was selfishly delighted to get away from the Home and honestly felt my lovable sister May would be OK—she and Myrtle were together. But she was not all right; she fretted so much. I realised years later how sensitive she was. I believe she was very sick after I left. Myrtle seemed to be OK and was sent to that white Home the girls spoke of. That was the last straw for my dear, fretting sister May.

I have often wondered how many of these children fretted and were like my sister. I have also wondered how many descendants of these fair-skinned Aboriginal children ever returned to their kith and kin on their Aboriginal side. I wonder how many have forgotten that they came from Black relations marrying other nationalities, wiping out their inheritance unknowingly. Probably they would be brainwashed into thinking colour did matter and character didn't. I will never cease being grateful to real sincere Christian people who showed me—by their standard of living—that it was not colour that counted. Character is the most important issue.

However, after Beatrice and I arrived at Sydney railway station, two policemen took us to the police station (I don't know why they needed two policemen). It was early morning. When the day-shift policemen arrived, we were put into the care of one and taken to the Protection Board office, where our mistresses were to call and collect us. That was the last I saw of Beatrice, although years later her brother married a Victorian girl. She is a great-grandmother now. She is a descendant of old Aunty Mary Clark in Purnim, near Warrnambool, the third generation from Granny Truganini of Tasmania. Jim Berg, Beatrice's grandson, married my father's sister's granddaughter, Margaret Freeman. We loved her father, Pat Freeman, very much. Jim is a dedicated worker for his race; he is the president of the Aboriginal Legal Aid, and attends many courts where many unfortunate Aboriginals' needs are to be pleaded for. Margaret, Jim's wife, is a leader in many Aboriginal organisations and they have three fine teenage children, one boy and two girls. I am very proud of them all.

The young constable left Beatrice and I at the Aborigines Protection Board office. I cannot even say that we were offered a cup of tea after that long journey from Cootamundra. However, our mistresses called for us, and Beatrice went off with her lady. That was when my heart was heavy. It was fun while we were together. Now I was on my own in this big city with white people whom I had never lived with before. A deep loneliness settled on me. I was scared for the first time.

I realised we were dressed in things that made us look older than we were. I realised that a lot would be expected of me now. But it was a sham! I did not know the first thing about the way white people lived.

Then my mistress came to collect me. My heart lifted from fright because she was rather pretty (I thought every white lady was pretty who had pretty clothes). She was attractive and she greeted me quite friendly. She said that she would not be taking me home right away but was taking me to stay at a private hospital to look after her baby boy, aged about twelve months. He was ill and missed the other Aboriginal girl whose place I was taking. 'Oh, she was a pretty Aboriginal girl', my mistress told me, and 'Oh this little boy loved her and is going to miss her'. I thought to myself, 'Oh, joy, a little baby'. We all loved babies and I was sure this baby would love me too.

I was taken to sit beside this little fellow in the cot. He was a lovely baby, but he just didn't take any notice of me! He was a very sick little fellow. When no-one else was in the room, just he and I, I did my best to amuse him and have him take notice of me. So, I just sat there too, and played or fingered his toys. I cannot remember how many days I was there, foisted onto this sick little fellow, who probably wanted his own Black nurse that he loved. Eventually, he was taken home, and I with him. There I met his two older sisters, Mauvely, three, and Elizabeth, nearly five. I was painfully shy, especially of the master of the house, who was English and a gentleman.

Chapter Nine

I cannot quite recall every detail of those first few days in Beecroft Road, Cheltenham. The trains ran down beyond the bottom of the garden fence to and from Sydney, meeting up with other trains from other cities. How I longed to be in one of them taking me back to my people!

I am sure it must have been difficult to teach me the way to care for that beautiful home, in which I did not have one scrap of interest. I cannot imagine how I got through the first few weeks and months. I was confused, shy and fretted for my people. At first, I was used mostly as a nurse girl, which made me feel more at ease. After a while, I was trusted to mind the baby boy out in the big garden. Actually the children helped me through the heartbreaking loneliness. It is a natural instinct for Aborigines to love children, so I was happier when I was with those three lovable little ones. And they were all my shadows. Elizabeth was highly strung and chatted incessantly, liking to boss the show. As she grew older, she recognised that I was a servant for her benefit, but I was the first one she would run to for comfort if she was hurt. She was really a lovely child. Mauvely was an adorable child and I felt she sensed when I was homesick, because she would toddle around with me as I weeded the garden or fed the chooks.

Chapter Nine

The little boy and I were inseparable. I carried him here and there until he learned to toddle. As well as looking after the children, I learned to do all sorts of work, mainly outside: garden work, feeding the poultry, mixing their food. There were chicks and ducklings hatched by incubator. When I dug the weeds in the garden with my fork or hand-trowel, I had the ducklings scrambling over my hands, gobbling up the worms. It would be great fun for me, and the children would all giggle with me. The ducklings were kept in the tool shed at night. They would nestle up together, such pretty, fluffy little things, till one morning there was a tragedy and we found some of them mutilated by rats. The big shed had an earthen floor and the boss and his wife searched for those wretched rat holes. When they found the holes, they poured kettles of boiling water down them. Out came the jumping, screaming rats. I don't know who screamed more, the lady or the rats. Mr Smith had to go to the rescue and kill the rats with an iron bar, so they wouldn't scream anymore. I was glad, as I felt it was a cruel way to kill anything. Later on, they bought some tins of stuff that looked like white ointment. It was called *Rough on Rats*. He spread it on slices of bread, cut them into squares, and put some into each hole. The tin of *Rough on Rats* was then put high up on a shelf, away from the children. I don't remember seeing any dead rats.

My mistress must have thought it was time I learned the housework. I did my very best, but try as I might, I could not please her. Her house had the name of being the cleanest, shiniest house for miles around, and I believed it! But she was also the most nerve-wracked woman around as well. She was worse than Miss Wood at Cootamundra. But I did not have anyone else to share the knocks with in Cheltenham. I discovered I could not please her. I was not good at housework, not the way she wanted it anyway. The only thing I was good at was keeping the children out of her way, so that she would not get at them.

I realise now that she must have been pretty sick in her mind. She was training the little boy to leave off nappies and use the toilet, and he would cry with fright when he forgot. Then she would smack him.

I couldn't stand it when she gave him one of those awful hard smacks. After all, he was only a baby still.

One day, I was weeding a bed of prize chrysanthemums. They were all staked up high, and were very bushy. When I heard this little fellow crying and calling my name, I called out to him. He was shaking with fear. I picked him up and said, 'What's the matter, love?' I soon knew. His fear of his mother was so great and so was mine. Fortunately it was a hot day. He had on those tussore silk panties, and I washed them out under the tap and hung them on the chrysanthemum bushes to dry. I kept him hidden from view in his little short shirt till his pants were dry. Anyway, he didn't get belted.

My mistress tried to teach me to wash. I wanted to learn because I like washing down by the river with plenty of soapy water, heated in a kerosene tin. That's how Mother and old Aunt did it. But this house had troughs and taps to turn on water, and a copper. Half the time, there was not enough wood, or there were only big blocks that I tried to split with a blunt axe. I didn't like washing days in Cheltenham. I was expected to wash the dirty nappies, some of which I had hidden from my mistress in case the little fellow would be spanked. I know now how wrong it was. On this particular day, she found the pile of messy [nappies]. I was horrified inside and prayed the little fellow was not near. I knew she loved him in some sort of way, of course. She grabbed me by the hair and threw all those dirty nappies over me.

I fought like mad. I don't know where I got the strength from. She was trying to rub them on my face. Anyone can guess what they looked like and smelt like and felt like. For the first time, I felt a deep resentment. But I had saved that little fellow from a spanking. I know now it was the wrong way to do it. I refused point blank to help her with the washing until I had scrubbed myself with buckets of water. Then she came out and turned the hose on me. Sometimes when she was in a good mood she would spray the children with the hose on a hot day, and she would turn it on me too. I didn't mind and the little ones thought it was great fun.

Chapter Nine

I shall never forget when my mistress's old mother and father and sister came from Moss Vale to stay. They were very kind and I was miserable when they left. I was treated and fed better when they were visiting.

I learned to be a good man-of-all-work in the garden. I mowed the lawns as good as the next, and there were huge areas to mow. One lawn was a tennis court although no-one played on it. It took some mowing and was heavy work for a homesick Aborigine on a light diet. The children loved playing on the lawns, and in the sand down at the bottom of the garden under the shady trees where the swings were. I used to love swinging them, and it was a happy playing corner and sort of sanctuary for me as well. The mistress would, of course, be keeping her eye on us from the many windows of the house.

I was constantly empty and I was always thinking how I could get food from the pantry. For play lunch, the children would be given a slice of bread, with butter or jam. They were very well fed and would take only a couple of mouthfuls and discard it. Sometimes I would encourage them to go and ask for some more, and they learned to share it with me. Then their mother asked why the children were always running back for more bread and butter. Bless them, they were innocent enough to say they wanted some for me, so that was the end of it.

I used to look forward to the postman's whistle. He was a dear old fellow with a long black beard and thick black hair. He was a genuine, kindly and cheerful man. He did his rounds on horseback and was never too busy to say a kind word to me. He would always greet the children too and they loved him and so did I. I would always be praying there was a letter for me. He would say, 'No letter', or 'There is a letter for you, Missy'. He made me feel like a person. He was the bringer of news from my people. We would hear his whistle up the street, and rush to the front gate to wait for him and pat his horse. On one particular day, he gave me a letter and said, 'Here is a letter for you, Missy'. I dared not open it before my mistress saw it but, with a thrilling, happy expectation, I took it to her. She had been watching through the window. She took the letter as I said happily, 'A letter from my mother'. My mother has long since joined her tribe in Dreamtime, but I can still remember her handwriting, which people used to say was beautiful, and she spelled perfectly, they said.

I waited expectantly for my letter to be given [to] me. That day passed, a week, a month. I had forgotten about food in my longing for that letter. I wept. I was too afraid to even mention it. I daren't, as I sensed she may have read something in it that she didn't agree with, and would take it out on me. Oh God, how I prayed for that letter and hungered for news of home, which seemed as far away as another planet. It was like a disease. A day never passed without me thinking, 'Oh, she'll give it to me today'. I couldn't write home because I depended on her for a stamped envelope and writing paper. Normally I was cunning enough to ask for it when her husband was home in the evening. She would read every word of the letter I wrote before it was posted.

One day she and another lady took their children to Sydney for the day. She locked up the house and gave me jobs to keep me busy all day: digging in the garden, mowing the lawns, cleaning the shed and raking the poultry yard. I watched them out of sight and then saw the train go to the city. My blackfellow cunning, as she used to describe it, came to the surface. I wondered how I could get into that house to search for the letter. The windows all had wire screens and although I discovered one of the windows at the back of the house was open, the screen was firmly in place. I wouldn't give up. I studied the bolt and went into the shed where the tools were kept. I found something I thought would do the job. And so I achieved my first and only house breaking and entering. I am puzzled still about who helped me, God or the devil. I firmly believe it wasn't the devil. I unbolted that long window screen and jumped through with ease. I had a frightened feeling. I had this whole place to myself. It was wrong, but I consoled myself with the thought that my mistress was wrong too in keeping my letter. My instinct led me to her bedroom. I searched the drawers and put back everything carefully. I thought, 'Oh, God, don't let me fail'. And then I remembered people often put things under their pillows or the mattress. I lifted up her mattress and there was my letter! I cannot describe the feeling of joy as I grabbed it and held it. She hadn't opened it! I sat on the floor at the foot of her bed and cried and cried. Then I put the letter back under the mattress, straightened the bed and made my way out through the window, bolting the screen again. Later, I asked my mistress when she was in a good mood if I could write a letter to my mother. She took her time finding the paper and envelope, and then she brought to light my mother's letter. I honestly feel she had forgotten. I wrote home, but couldn't tell Mother of my deep need, and of the happenings. I could only draw things that happened. I liked to do this. Mother got the letter and was horrified by what she read in the drawings.

Miserable days turned into weeks—months—then years. I was just sixteen years old, tall, skinny and growing more cunning, but not cunning enough in pinching food. Every chance I had, I took a little something from the pantry. There wasn't much of a selection either, only jams and sugar, or the usual uncooked commodities. The shelves were crowded with homemade jams and I would hide them under the house. They came in handy because Mrs S would give me the leftover porridge, when there was any, without milk or sugar. I would eat it, but ugh! So, the jam made a lot of difference.

I feel awful when I think of those days and what thieving I was practising. God seemed so far away, like my mother and father, aunt, uncle and sisters—in fact, all my Aboriginal people. Winter and summer came and went. I was always dressed scantily in a thin blouse, skirt and a hessian or sugar bag singlet that she made; no underclothing and my legs and feet were bare. She had to clothe me, so I suppose I was an expense. But in wintertime, oh, the cold was unbearable. I would wait for the first streak of sun and I would stand in that spot, or where the sun shifted. Yes, I learned how much that sun was my friend. When it was covered in cloud, or when it was frosty in the cold season, I would sit in the shed. If there were bags or such things, I would cover myself over to keep warm. This was in the morning. I had to get up early to make my bed and get them a cup of tea. I would snatch a cup of tea. Then they would get up. The boss had to go to work. Then I wouldn't be allowed inside all day. Taking a cup of tea to them in the morning then stopped, because I put too much milk in my own tea. I did too! And of course, then they didn't have any milk for their breakfast. So, tea went off my diet as well.

I looked forward so much to her brother-in-law and sister from Queensland visiting because she couldn't lose face in not dishing up a meal for me. It is a true saying that you find your way to the heart of a person through his or her stomach. Well, I loved everyone in that house while I was being fed. The brother-in-law was a very quiet man. I was afraid of him; I was always very shy of white men. His wife, I thought, was beautiful and kind. She always slipped a cup of tea and lunch to me outside. I became an expert at cleaning boots and shoes, which I had to every day, so I did her brother-in-law's as well. Well, those two weeks had to end, and those good folks had to go. The morning they were going, the brother-in-law took a stroll outside with the children. I was so thrilled when he said thank you for cleaning his boots every morning. Then he gave me five shillings. My heart was overflowing. A little later, he and his wife came out and kindly said goodbye, and he gave me another half-crown. Oh, I thought I was rich. A funny thing, I went straight to the shed and hid the five shillings where I hid my mother's letters, to read them when I felt lonely. I don't know what made me put the half-crown in another place. However, as soon as the brother-in-law and sister went, my mistress came to me and said, 'Give me the money my brother-in-law gave you'. She must have asked him if he had given me something. I think that is why he gave me the second lot, which I had hidden in a separate place. She said I had to pay for things I broke, cups and things. I was miserable as I handed her the half-crown, hoping she would not know about the five shillings, and she didn't. I thanked God and hid the other money in a safer place until I could use it, which happened to be sooner than I expected.

Chapter Nine

When I look back to those years, oh my! I was getting cunning and what an obsession I had with food! I wondered how I was going to obtain food with that gift of five shillings. The nearest shop was one mile or so away at Epping and I didn't have a hope of being let out on my own. Then, out of the blue, I was sent to Epping on an urgent message for my mistress. I assured her that I would go straight there and back. Didn't I enjoy that walk! There was timber and shrubs, and I felt the freedom of being alone, being trusted. It did not enter my head to run away or any other such thing. As I clutched that five shillings tied in a piece of rag, I thought and wondered what eats I could buy with it. I soon made up my mind: rock cakes or some other cakes. I couldn't get home quick enough to eat them. I ate a couple walking back, and said happily to myself, 'I'll keep some for tomorrow and for as long as I can. I won't need to pinch anything'. There wasn't much hope of that. My mistress seemed to know my every move. Just before I arrived at the front gate, I saw a thick, well-kept hedge along the front fence. I felt it was a good hiding place. So, before I entered the gate, I put about half a dozen of my luscious cakes in their paper bag (they were luscious to me, anyway) [and] hid them in the garden hedge. Then I went contentedly through the gate. And, oh, the front door opened and out she came! I knew by the look on her face that something was not going to be good for me. Then, oh no, she had been watching me through the window as per usual. She just said to me, 'Follow me', which I did. She opened the gate. She knew exactly where to get my bag of cakes. She went back through the gate again and down the drive with me still following her, anxious about my rock cakes. Then she detoured down the path to the fowl yard and went through the gate, me still following her. She stopped in the middle of the fowl yard, where the ducks, bantams and fowls clustered around thinking it was feeding time, although it was the wrong time of the day. She took a rock cake out of the bag and deliberately broke [it] up into little pieces. My feelings were mixed; I felt I couldn't win, so why did I keep on trying? I couldn't believe my eyes: the whole lot of those fowls just picked casually at a piece of cake here, a piece of cake there, and then just walked away. I thought, 'My goodness, fancy knocking back my lovely cakes'. The truth dawned on me sometime later; they were better fed than I was. They were used to being fed with proper meals. Then, without a word, she marched out of the fowl yard, leaving me standing there. When she was out of sight, I hunted the chooks away and picked up some of the bigger pieces of cake. I put the pieces in the paper bag that she had thrown on the ground. I can remember, no matter how hungry we used to be at Moonahcullah, we did not pick things off the ground to eat them. It did enter my head to wonder why she disliked me so; I got so used to her calling me a 'wretched black thing', not realising I was one.

I could never win.

One day, another hungry day for a growing fifteen-and-a-half-year-old girl, I was told by my mistress to get the rake and old broom and the wheelbarrow. I was to clean out the fowl houses and to rake up the fowl yard—rather a good-sized yard. As usual, I had not been given breakfast. Yes, I was hungry, but I drew the line at eating the chooks' pollard and bran. As I raked, I was thinking of stews, bread and butter or jam, or even the good old bread and dripping. I stopped raking for a minute's rest, keeping an eye on the gate for my mistress, who had the knack of popping up at the wrong moment. I guess she didn't trust me. As I watched the antics of those chooks and ducks, I thought, 'Gee it would be good to have one of you on the coals'. But they all looked at me trustingly, with their heads sideways, clucking away in chooks' language. Anyway, a bright thought came to me. I raked all the rubbish straw out of the nest into little heaps here and there, which I then burnt, and then put clean straw into the nests. I remembered there were some eggs in the nests. So, still keeping an eye on the gate, I sneaked (awful word, but I did, I sneaked) into the fowl house and collected about half-a-dozen eggs. I put one egg into each of those little fires burning the rubbish and covered them over carefully with the hot ashes. I raked away cheerfully in anticipation of a feed at last. Just when I thought they would surely be finished, there was the mistress coming through the gate, so I started to rake the yard like mad. She stood and looked around to see if I left anything unraked. I was feeling so pleased with myself. I was very meek, and I asked if there was anything else that I could rake. Everything was well done, and I was longing to have a feed of those gorgeous googies, and yet she lingered for just a half a minute more. I was feeling that I was not safe yet. Just as she turned to go and stepped around a little burning heap, those eggs started to pop quite loudly. My hunger left me; all I was thinking was, 'She will kill me!' Well, she took the rake and went to all those little heaps, raked the eggs out and smashed them. I did wonder if the good Lord was teaching me a lesson for stealing those eggs. Thou shalt not steal. I should have said, 'Those eggs are just a drop in the ocean compared to the whole of my country, which you took': wishful thinking.

So many awful experiences I have gone through. I often wonder if it has taught us something; yes, I feel it has. It has taken me a long time to see that, in spite of it all, bitterness and hate is not the answer. Caring for people, rich or poor, goes a long way to righting wrongs. I do feel what happened to me in my youth was an experience I shall do my best to forget, and not keep it sizzling in my heart. I am not bitter, but feel this experience has not only been mine. Many black children, and maybe white children, experienced similar.

One day, I was minding the children down the bottom of the garden, where there was a sandpit and a two-seated swing. When the kiddies got tired of playing in the sand, I would put them on the swing and I stood on the platform between the two seats. They were not meant to go too high, and I watched them carefully. However, I did not watch myself, and as one seat used to go down and the other up, one of the seats scraped my shinbone pretty hard. I thought my leg was broken. I cried with the pain, the little ones watching me in sympathy. The oldest one was trying to tell her mother, but I said it was OK; feeling my mistress would not let me swing the children anymore. I tried not to limp when she was near. One day, she and another lady across the street made up their minds to take the children to the zoo; they would take me along to mind them. Any other time, the day would have been wonderful, I would have been thrilled, as I felt I had the chance to be given something to eat at the picnic when others were present. I hid my limp as best I could. It was the days when black stockings were worn; when my leg started to bleed, the black dye did its work and the stocking stuck to my leg. When we got home, I tried to get my stocking off, but it was painfully attached to the sore. When I eventually pulled the stocking off, the sore was pretty deep and running. I had no rag, and it was ugly-looking and painful, because my skirt rubbed against it. So, in desperation, I tied my black stocking around it. However, it got worse and I could not hide my limp anymore. The mistress asked me why I was limping. There was nothing I could do but to show my sore leg. As I pulled back the black cotton stocking that I had used for a bandage, she took one look at the sore, which was a pretty deep hole, gave a gasp and ran out of the room. She gave the doctor a call. I was still sitting out on the garden seat, which was near the kitchen door, when the doctor came. I don't know what she told the doctor, but she said to me later (whether it was true or not) that if the wound was another fraction deeper, it would have been on the bone and I would have had to have my leg cut off. She also said that the doctor said that Aborigines had no feeling anyway, we were like animals, our wounds just healed without any trouble. It didn't worry me; things could have been worse anyhow. I had to sit every day for nearly a week under the trees, out the back, on that garden seat with my leg up. She brought the dishes out to me to wash up. I cleaned the silver, peeled the vegetables, all because the doctor said I was not to use the leg. Oh, she grudgingly gave me food such as broth, because the doctor said that I was to have it. However, the children kept me company. I never told her how that sore started. I suppose it would not have made a difference anyway.

One morning, I was washing up outside, sitting down with my leg up. I did not do something properly. She was in a bad mood, and I copped it, as the saying goes. She boxed my ears as she held me by the hair. She slapped my face, as I cried, 'Don't, you are hurting'. She was like a mad person. She did not stop until her husband came to the door and begged her to stop, because she was upsetting herself. As I fell off the seat, bad leg and all, I started to yell and cry. Her husband said, 'Oh dear, can't you stop her, the neighbours will hear her'. So, being given the idea, I did just that! I yelled and yelled and screamed. She threw water on me. Still I yelled. She said she would call the police. I felt nothing could be worse than this, so I still yelled and screamed. Then I saw that the two little kiddies, the girl four-and-a-half and then the little boy, had come out of the house and were screaming and crying for me. Then I shut up. I cuddled them and said, 'Don't cry, don't cry, I am alright'. I got my leg better and I didn't get hit for a long time; in fact, other tactics were being used.

When we girls were sent out to the situations from the Homes, we were not given many clothes to come away with. Our mistresses had to clothe us. Hence my first experience wearing a hessian bag singlet, a winceyette shirt, a print blouse and nothing else. Maybe I was hard on clothes. Then she put me into cast-off trousers of the bosses. This would not have mattered these days, but I was ashamed and spent my time hiding every time a tradesman came. Once, when the younger milkman came in to collect money, I just had time to run around the high chrysanthemums. He must have glimpsed me and wondered who the new black boy was. He was not satisfied; he had to chase me around that bed of chrysanthemums. I was so indignant; I rushed for the toilet, where I shut myself in, away from his grinning face.

Time went on. Then one day, my mother came.

I had drawn pictures on my last letter; signs of what was happening, as only a mother can guess and see things. She braved that long journey to that big unknown city, finding the headquarters of the Australian Inland Mission and the Reverend Long. His work as the head of AIM, as far as I can remember, was known and welcomed everywhere. So, my mother found him and his family in Sydney and poured her heart out to him. Straight away he took her to the Aborigines Protection Board office, where she poured out her heartbreaking story of how she believed I was being treated. My mistress later told me that the Aborigines Protection Board called my mother 'that woman'. Even poor old Reverend Long was inclined to think that my mother was unnecessarily worried, as the board told her she had 'absolutely nothing to worry about'.

I will never forget that particular day my mother came. My mistress went out of her way to be nice to her, and to me. I had been given decent clothes to put on the day before. Her excuse was I had to have the others washed. I still had my winceyette skirt and print blouse, but for the first time in a long time I was told to wear my boots instead of going bare-footed.

My mother must have been a good tracker, because she found this home where I was. This particular day, I was down the bottom of the yard with the little children, amusing them, playing in the sand or giving them a swing. My mistress came down with a plate of eats and some milk, and she gave me some as well—unheard of! I was grateful for the eats, I accepted [them] with wonder and delight. Then she joined in with the children, making little sandcastles. The children were delighted. I giggled, wondering what was going to happen next! Then she abruptly stopped swinging us, and started going towards the front gate, where there was a woman standing and waving. And she was dark! I just caught the words my mistress said as she walked away from us, 'You stay there with the children', which I thought was a funny thing to say. It did not take me long to wake up and understand. As I gazed at the person at the gate who was waving to us, slowly, my dullness cleared, and I realised it was my mother.

Oh, the joy! I can feel it as I write—I experienced it. I kept thinking, 'How! How did she find me? How did she manage it?' as I watched in that second and as I think of it now. As I think of her now, I cry. I cannot help it. I think of all mothers, and my wonderful Aboriginal mother finding her way from the bush. She read my drawings of a figure chasing a smaller black figure, hitting the black figure on the head with the saucepan.

I did not realise that my mistress was trying to stop her coming to see me. Mother was waving her arms about. I felt so afraid that she

Chapter Nine

Page 1 of 'The day Mother came' from Margaret's handwritten manuscript.

would get into trouble if I went to her. I thought, 'Oh, please God, don't let her be hurt. It's my fault she is here, if I go to her it will make things worse'. But she did come to me. My mistress was no match for a worried mother who had her children taken from her. As she came to where I was standing with the children, my whole being catapulted to meet her. Tears ran down both our faces. She stroked my head and said, 'How tall you have grown'. I giggled nervously and said, 'Mum—you here'. I don't know how my mother did it, but she was allowed to stay the night with me. With all the happenings, my mistress was still worrying about not having tea ready in time for her husband. I can remember Mother asking her for an apron and she helped her get the master's tea on time.

Between tea and bedtime, my mistress told Mother how naughty and hard-headed I was. She said that she might get into trouble for having Mother stay. However, Mother did stay. We talked, and being a woman of faith, she prayed to God for help. I felt things would be righted; I felt somewhat miserable and ashamed for the unhappiness I had created for her. But, oh, I was happy and joyful that she was with me. I just couldn't think about what was going to happen afterwards. I told her everything, showed her the scars on my body. As I think now, I am filled with remorse for doing so, but I did not know my mother very much. I had so much fear of the white people's power and was terrified for my Aboriginal people. I didn't know the answer to it all. I vaguely wondered why God had forsaken us Black people, what good were we? Me especially?

Mother went to the city next morning, after first asking if she could do something to help; she always showed a giving spirit. The next few days seemed to come and go, and my mistress was getting back to her usual form. Perhaps seeing my mother may have spoilt me a bit, but I was still up in the clouds because Mother said that she was going to try to beg the Aborigines Protection Board to let me go home with her. It certainly was a big hope (well, it was for me) that did not materialise. Mother did turn up again, and not alone. My father was with her. I was down at the bottom of the garden in the sand pit again with the children and, like a vision, my mistress was at the gate. As I watched, she led my mother and father down to the sandpit and the swing. I did not have boots or shoes on this day, and I felt a bit ashamed, as my mother and father (especially Father) were dressed well. He was a well-known shearer and could afford to dress well. He was still a roamer, and Mother had tracked him down. I tried to dig my toes into the sand to hide my feet.

I was shy of my father; he was rather a handsome man and six-feet four or five. Mother was a tall woman, but she looked tiny beside him. I greeted him, but still conscious of my bare feet and how I was dressed. I think my mistress was too. She stood talking to my parents, they could hardly get a word to me; but I do remember my father offering me two half crowns. Oh my, I was thrilled. Then the mistress said, 'No, Margaret has plenty of everything, she doesn't need it'. I felt like yelling, 'I do need it, I do!' I watched my father's hands, still holding the half crowns. My mother was telling my mistress something—I can't remember exactly what—taking my mistress's attention away for a few seconds. My goodness, we must have been shifty people. Anyway, my father dropped the two half-crowns where he was standing. His boot moved some sand over them, as I watched, fascinated. Then he gave me a quick glance and a wink to see if I'd seen what had happened. I saw what happened all right. I feel a bit of shame when I think of some of the shifty things I had to get up to, just to exist. I cannot remember how I spent those two lovely silver half-crowns.

That was not all, my mistress told me that the Protection Board phoned her a day or so later. They said that 'that man and woman' were creating a terrible disturbance, wanting to take me home. From what my mistress said, I knew there was no hope, so I went back to my old routine. I was tall and thin; may I be forgiven for feeling miserable and hopeless? I had turned sixteen and longed for freedom with my people. Seeing my mother and father made things worse, not knowing when I would see them again. I lost all sense of time. I suffered more indignities. I don't know why she would get so cross with me when I would least expect it. She would take great delight (it seemed to me) in making me

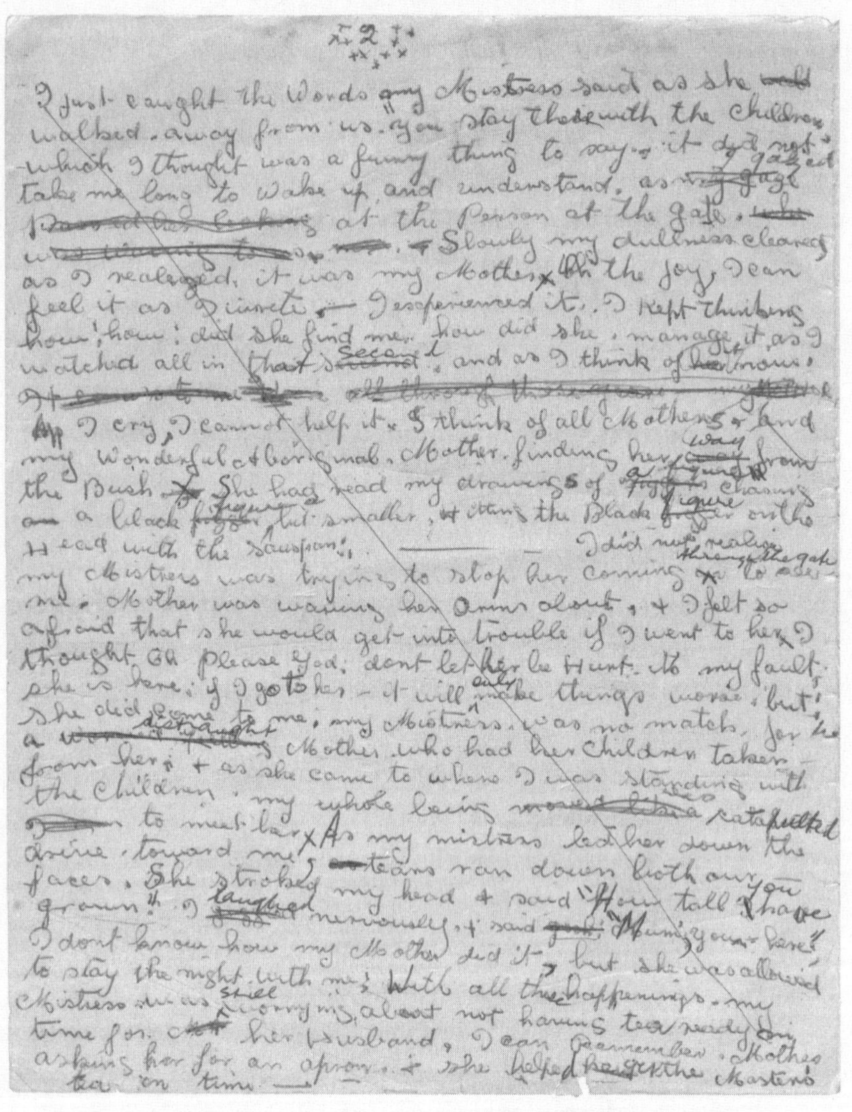

2

I just caught the Words my Mistress said as she
walked away from us. "You stay there with the children"
which I thought was a funny thing to say. It did not
take me long to wake up and understand, as I gazed
[illegible] at the Person at the gate. [illegible]
[illegible]. Slowly my dullness cleared
as I realized, it was my Mother. Oh the joy, I can
feel it as I [illegible] I experienced it. I kept thinking
how, how, did she find me. How did she manage it, as I
watched all in that second, and as I think of it now.
[illegible]
I cry, I cannot help it. I think of all Mothers & kind
my wonderful Aboriginal Mother finding her way from
the Bush. She had read my drawings of a figure chasing
a black figure but smaller, hitting the Black figure on the
Head with the saucepan!, ——— — I did not realize
my Mistress was trying to stop her coming through the gate to see
me. Mother was waving her Arms about, & I felt so
afraid that she would get into trouble if I went to her. I
thought Oh Please God, dont let her be Hurt. Its my fault
she is here, if I go to her – it will only make things worse, but
She did come to me, my Mistress was no match for the
a distraught Mother who had her Children taken
from her, & as she came to where I was standing with
the Children, my whole being [illegible] catapulted
to meet her. As my mistress led her down the
drive, toward me, tears ran down both our
faces. She stroked my head & said "How tall you have
grown!" I laughed nervously, & said "Mum, your here!"
I dont know how my Mother did it, but she was allowed
to stay the night with me. With all the happenings, my
Mistress was still worrying about not having tea ready on
time for her Husband, I can Remember Mother
asking her for an apron, & she helped get the Master's
tea on time ———

Page 2 of 'The day Mother came' from Margaret's handwritten manuscript.

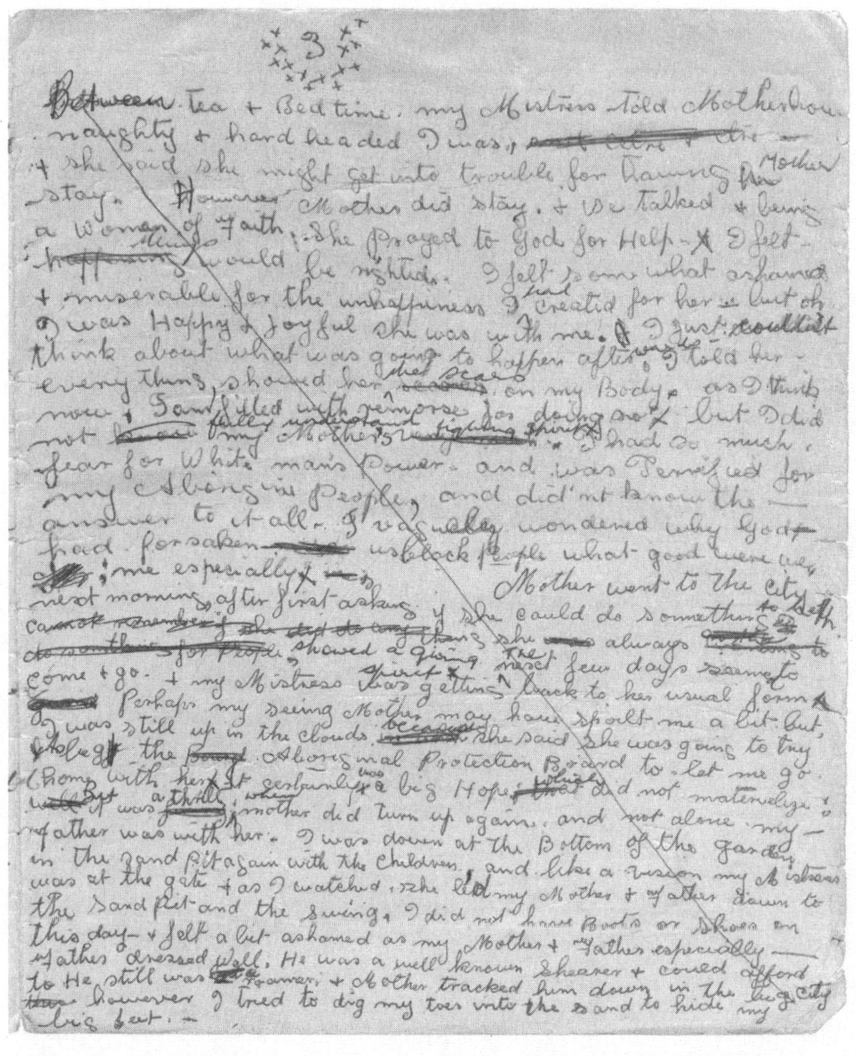

3

Between Tea + Bed time. my Mistress Told Mother how naughty + hard headed I was, + she said she might get into trouble for having Mother stay. However Mother did stay. + we talked + being a Woman of Faith; She prayed to God for Help – + I felt things would be righted. I felt some what ashamed + miserable for the unhappiness I had created for her – but oh I was Happy + Joyful she was with me. + I just couldn't think about what was going to happen after wards. I told her every thing, showed her the scars on my Body. as I think now, I am filled with remorse for doing so, but I did not fully understand my Mother's fighting spirit. + I had so much fear for White man's Power – and was Terrified for my Aboriginal People, and did'nt know the answer to it all. I vaguely wondered why God had forsaken us black People what good were we; me especially.

Mother went to the city next morning, after first asking if she could do something to help [illegible] for People, showed a giving spirit. she always [illegible] The next few days seemed to come + go. + my Mistress was getting back to her usual form. Perhaps my seeing Mother may have spoilt me a bit but, I was still up in the clouds, because she said she was going to try the Aboriginal Protection Board to let me go home with her. It certainly was a big Hope, which did not materialize. But it was a thrill when mother did turn up again, and not alone – my father was with her. I was down at the Bottom of the garden in the sand pit again with the Children, and like a vision my Mistress was at the gate + as I watched, she led my Mother + Father down to the Sand pit and the swing. I did not have Boots or Shoes on this day – + felt a bit ashamed as my Mother + my Father especially – Father dressed well, He was a well known Shearer + could afford to. He still was a Roamer, + Mother tracked him down in the big City however I tried to dig my toes into the sand to hide my big feet. –

Page 3 of 'The day Mother came' from Margaret's handwritten manuscript.

strip and then turning the hose on me, in front of men working on a building next to the property. Fortunately, I didn't hear any insults from them, but I just wanted to die, nothing mattered anymore.

I started thinking, 'What is the best way to have an accident to end it all?' I thought of getting over the tall paling fence at the bottom of the fowl yard, then down to the train line where the country trains and goods trains came and went all day. Well, the passenger trains travelled too fast, but the goods train was slow coming up the hill from the city. So, I toyed with the idea of having a broken leg or something, then they would have to send me home because I could not work anymore. The thought fascinated me for a day or so. After a belting or having my hair pulled out, I sneaked down to the railway line. Some suburban trains went past. I let them, they frightened me: they were going too fast. But I heard the slow shunting of the goods train, which seemed to struggle up the incline. I crept nearer to the train line and thought, 'Oh, I must not be frightened'. Believe me, I was scared, but I crept quite near; when the two train firemen yelled and bellowed at me to 'Get the bloody hell out of it'. Believe me, I did. I didn't stop running till I was back over the fence and into the fowl yard. I prayed that those men wouldn't tell on me, but I need not have worried, I didn't hear anything of it.

I started to think up something else. I was just too miserable for words. I could not do anything right, or anything to please her. I feel now that I was fretting for home after seeing Mother and Father. I was like a crazy person. It was a Sunday, I remember because the little girls were with their father, who was amusing them. The little boy was asleep. I thought of something, it became an obsession with me. I wondered what could make me ill. I didn't want to die; I just wanted to be ill and to go home. So, the wicked plan came to me to take *Rough on Rats*. I knew where they hid the tin of it. I got it down. This was all happening after a Sunday dinner; in which I was included, the boss being home. I remember how I loved eating the younger cooked carrots, which were a bit salty. I rolled two little bits of *Rough on Rats* into a soft ball, small enough to swallow, which I did. That moment, my mistress, who had long hair, called me in to brush it. She did this when her husband was home playing with the children. I started to feel funny, my arms wouldn't work; and she protested angrily because my hand with the brush was just flopping on her head. Then my head and stomach were acting all funny and dizzy. I wanted to be sick, and told her what I had done. I staggered down to the backyard and, fortunately for me, I vomited and vomited. I fell, but crawled back to the kitchen steps a wreck, and I looked it. Meanwhile, of what I remember very vividly, she was ringing the doctor. She was very upset and got me into bed. The doctor said that the vomiting had saved me, but I felt that it was the salty carrots. Anyway, whatever it was, *Rough on Rats* was rough on me!

It was not long before the lady inspector from the Aboriginal Protection Board came out to see me. I was fond of her, she was always kind to me, but she didn't know how I was treated. I wouldn't tell her. She scolded me good and proper, and made me promise not to do such an awful thing again. She need not have worried; I had had it! I plucked up enough courage to say I could not please my mistress. She was standing quite near, and she put her arms around my shoulder and said, 'Oh, yes you can, Margaret dear'. Anyway, strangely enough, I was left alone, and I was given meals and was actually dressed for some weeks. Then one day a nurse friend of my mistress, who had an orchard of all kinds of fruit she used to bottle, asked my mistress if she could have me for a day to help her. Oh, I was thrilled when my mistress reluctantly said 'Yes'. I had to go to Pennant Hills; I ran to get the train and just caught it. I had a sneaking suspicion that my mistress didn't want me to catch that train, but I did. I found that I hadn't been given my fare; however, I was let off. I spent a lovely day with Nurse Field, who rang and told my mistress that I was a wonderful help. I cannot remember how it all happened, but my mother was engaged to work for the nurse and was allowed to have my little sister with her. She was ten years and some months old. I felt the good Lord was taking over at last—but another surprise: I was moved to another home. My new mistress was a motherly type, the wife of a cattleman from Goondiwindi.

Chapter Ten

Life with my new mistress and family was just the opposite to the last place. Mrs Pierce, a gentle ladylike person with six children, had lived on a cattle station somewhere near Goondiwindi. They had to move to the city because the children needed the best of schooling, which they got. She had five little children. One was born two days after I arrived, a little boy, whom I promptly took over. He was born on the day the Prince of Wales arrived in Sydney. We all went to see him land. I enjoyed it all, but I missed the little boy at the last place very much and the two little girls I had looked after at Cheltenham.

My mother was working in the city and on one of her first days off, she and my younger sister Geraldine came to see me in Neutral Bay. Mother asked my new mistress, who was a short motherly type, if I could go out with her and my little sister. To my amazement, I was allowed. Mother promised to bring me back again. As we got on the ferry, she said, 'I am taking you to see the children you used to love'. They had grown! and Mrs Smith was even pleased to see me, but she told me I had got too fat.

I learned a lot at that new place. They were an ordinary, happy, honest, old-fashioned family. I fitted in with them and was reasonably contented. I used to take the children for walks; at least they used to take

Chapter Ten

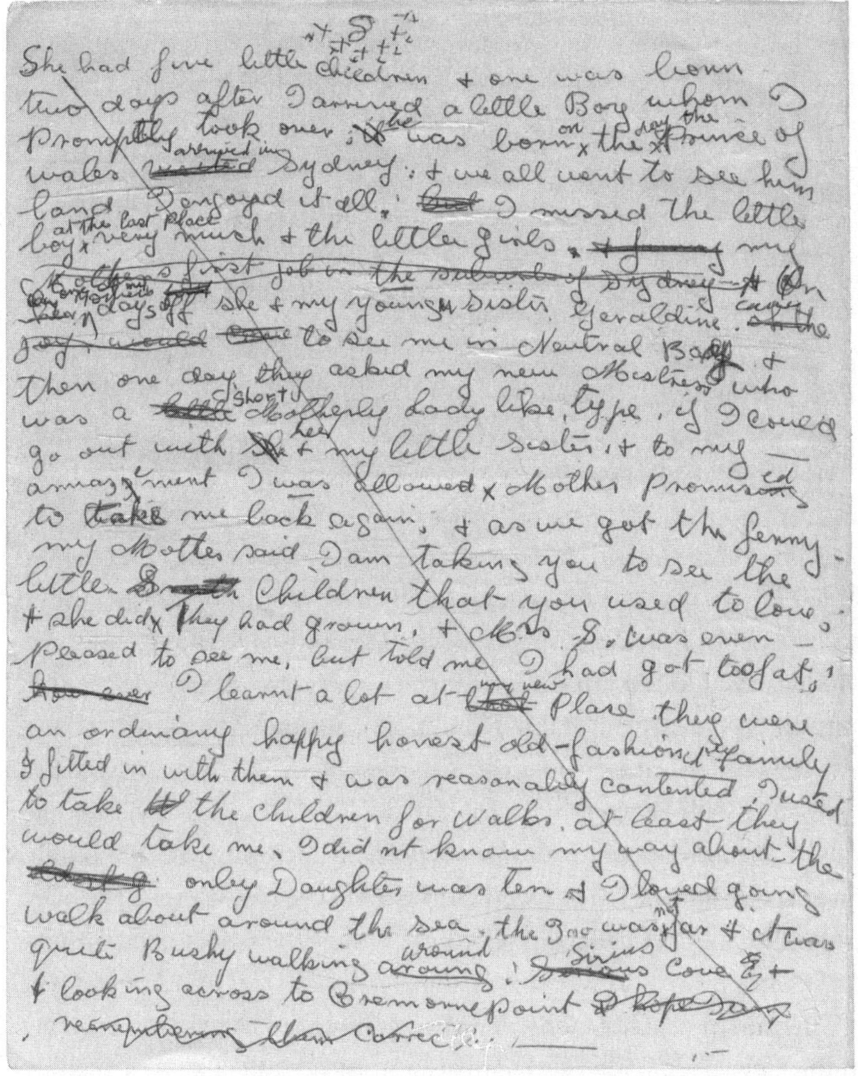

She had five little children + one was born
two days after I arrived a little Boy whom I
promptly took over; he was born on the day the Prince of
Wales arrived in Sydney: + we all went to see him
land I enjoyed it all, I missed the little
boy at the last place very much + the little girls,
On my days off she + my younger sister Geraldine came
to see me in Neutral Bay +
then one day they asked my new Mistress who
was a short + Motherly lady like type, if I could
go out with her + my little sister, + to my
amazement I was allowed + Mother promised
to take me back again, + as we got the ferry
my Mother said I am taking you to see the
little Children that you used to love,
+ she did they had grown, + Mrs S. was even
pleased to see me, but told me I had got too fat,
I learnt a lot at the new place they were
an ordinary happy honest old-fashioned family
I fitted in with them + was reasonably contented I used
to take the Children for walks, at least they
would take me, I did nt know my way about the
only Daughter was ten + I loved going
walk about around the sea, the Zoo was not far + it was
quite Bushy walking around Sirius Cove +
+ looking across to Bremonne point
correct.

Opening of Chapter Ten from Margaret's handwritten manuscript.

me, because I didn't know my way about the city. The only daughter was ten and I loved going walkabout with her around the sea. The zoo was not far, and it was quite bushy walking around Sirius Cove, looking across Cremorne Point.

They were a very wholesome family. In all my life since, I cannot remember living with a family like them. Mr Pierce, when he came home to his family from his cattle station in the less busy times, I liked right away. He was, I felt, straight and fair, and could see right through you. I used to hear him having a heart-to-heart talk with his children—especially his oldest son and daughter, aged eight and eleven. The girl was a fiery, bossy type and the boy was like his dad; and many a fight he got into over me, with his mates or others, because they called me 'blackfellow'. However, children will be children and mostly I find mostly they take the lead from how their family live.

For the first time, I learned what it was like to have a good three meals a day. I learned that there seemed to be no fear of the truth in this family. Of course, the children had their squabbles. For the first time, I had to call the children, small as they were, 'Miss' or 'Master'; from the ten year old down to the four year old, excepting the baby, who was four months old then. It didn't worry me—until going out on public outings with them. Then I would drop the 'Miss' or 'Master'. The boys wouldn't mind, but the ten-year-old girl did. I heard her complaining to her parents.

I didn't hear her mother saying anything, but her father was gently amused; but he gave her a straight answer, and a good talking to, making her see that she was still a little girl of ten years. It puzzled me and made me think. I was proud too; and although I was becoming very fond of the family, this 'Master' and 'Miss' to children brought it home to me that I was only a servant after all. It somehow reminded me of Uncle Tom's Cabin. However, I learned so many things there, and Mr P taught the children to always speak the truth—no matter what. So, they often got into mischief, but they did not defend themselves by telling a lie. This fascinated and appealed to me, so that when I broke an expensive article, I fought with my conscience for hours. I was terrified of owning up; but seeing and hearing those children owning up kept nagging at me.

At two o'clock in the morning, I heard the baby cry in his cot in his mother's room. I usually didn't pick him up at night, but now, for the first time, I got up, picked him up and changed him. Then I took him to another room and sang softly to him so as not to wake the others. He went to sleep, and I put him back in his cot. Mrs P was so pleased, and I told her the truth about breaking that article. All she said was, 'never mind, go to bed and sleep now'. I did. Later on, when he began to toddle, he used to come to my room and knock on the door and call 'Margareta'.

I was treated kindly; not like one of the family, but kindly. But something was missing. I was discontented. I was between seventeen and eighteen, and seeing and hearing what other Aboriginal girls that were in the Aboriginal Girls Home at Cootamundra were doing. My younger sister May, who was with me in the Home, had long since been sent out to service somewhere in Strathfield, a suburb of Sydney. Meanwhile, I put in for a couple of weeks holiday; to go home and see my people. I was thrilled when it was granted. It was great being with my people those couple of weeks and I very reluctantly returned to Sydney. It was very hard getting back into the work routine again. Then I had a visit from my Aunty May, my father's sister, a gentle, ladylike, attractive girl of about twenty years. She stayed the night. I liked her very much. She had been taken away and had been in Cootamundra Home a few years before May, Myrtle and I were taken there. She was sent out to service long before we arrived. Then I had a visit from my sister May, who had run away from the place where she was put to work. I got such a shock at my gentle, delicate sister doing such a thing! I felt admiration and thought I wasn't as courageous as she was. She came out to see me several times and I began to get discontented because I was missing so much so-called freedom. I was almost eighteen years of age. My dear little mistress was most kind and would let my sister stay the night and have tea. We would talk far into the night about all the fun she was having. She had found families of Aborigines and had met my father, who was pretty strict in the advice he gave her. A West Indian family gave her love and care; it was like a home away from home.

So, after these visits and chats, I made up my mind that I wasn't going to be Cinderella and stay home. I begged my reluctant sister to wait outside the front gate, which was a long way from the house. I would meet her after dark and go with her. She was working and had some money for fares. I had my pocket money that was always given to me by this mistress, and her husband was very generous when he was at home. I was pretty good at keeping the garden tidy, and he would give me a generous amount of pocket money. So, human nature what it is, I thoughtlessly, selfishly and excitedly climbed out of my bedroom window. Out the front gate, my sister was waiting for me. Oh, it was exciting. Going across [on] the ferry, I couldn't sit down. I stood holding the rails, watching the waves as the boat made its way across the harbour to Circular Quay. Then we made our way, me following my sister, to Woolloomooloo, where her coloured friends were. I noticed that they were very kind to May. It was a night that I will never forget. Her friend, a kind-hearted young woman of West Indian descent called Carrie, took us next door where there was a party on. I could hear the noise before getting to the place and was a bit apprehensive, but I trusted Carrie because May said that she was a nice girl. We got to this party, and I thought, 'Oh my', and had all sorts of feelings. It was a white person's home and it was filled with Samoan seamen. I think this woman's husband, Mr Adams, might have been on the same boat and had brought them home. There were about twenty of them: real big fellows. I had never had such an experience before. There were two Maoris there as well. I was very frightened at first, but Carrie told me they were all right, the lady of the house was her friend.

They were singing in their language in deep rich voices. I had not seen anything like it before. They were the most decent fellows one could meet. They tried to talk with us, but we couldn't understand each other's language. It was soon time to go home. The two Maori men had to catch the last ferry to North Shore. Not knowing anything about such things,

Carrie put me in their charge—May, my sister, taking her word that they were OK. My word, it was luck; we caught the last tram and the last ferry. But there were no trams on the other side around to Mosman or Neutral Bay. Undaunted, I said goodnight to the two Maoris (they had to get out to their ship in the middle of the harbour somewhere). I started to walk, I didn't know how far it was, I just thought to follow the tramline. However, one of the Maori boys chased after me and said it wouldn't be right for me to walk that distance at night on my own. I protested and said I was okay. To tell the truth, I was a bit fearful and shy of any man, but we talked about each other's race and country and customs, and we got used to each other. He said he would like to see me again. He did not appeal to me, apart from being a friend. I said I would see him again, and all of them, at Mrs Adams's home. I liked her and thought I'd go there again.

I climbed out the window again the next night when I thought everyone was asleep. I got the ferry to Circular Quay and the tram to Woolloomooloo. The people were nice and seemed glad to see me, and I felt free, or so I thought.

It was a bit frightening; I felt somehow that I was not playing the game properly. Anyway, I went home, catching the ferry boat and the last tram. That Maori boy came with me again. I did protest and told him that I knew my way home. However, I left him at the tram stop and told him to catch that tram back or he would have to walk, [so] he did. I hurried to get home, only to find all the lights on, including the one in my room, and the front door open. I was terrified. They would think that I was a bad girl and I would get sent to Parramatta Home for Bad Girls; where my old mistress said I would end up. Parramatta Home was where they dealt to bad girls exactly what they deserved. I didn't really know quite what I was doing, I just reached through the window of my room and grabbed another dress and a hat (I don't know why the hat) and I bolted again for the Mosman wharf to catch the ferry boat. Somehow, I got back to Carrie's home, but her people discouraged her from having me there when they found out that I had run away.

I didn't blame them. So, Carrie took me around to Mrs Adams. I sensed I wasn't welcome there either, but she didn't say so. The front door was wide open and, while we were talking, two big detectives walked past with the Maori men between them. We were all rooted to the spot. I could hardly breathe with fright. Fortunately, they went to Carrie's home first. Mrs Adams meanwhile tried all sorts of hiding places for me in the house, but it was no use. I was like a zombie; my brain wouldn't work at all. Then Mrs A took me out the back where there was a high brick wall. The backyard of another house was next to it, and next door to [that] was a vacant block with high grass growing. Poor Mrs A, swearing like a trooper, told me to climb over that wall and drop onto the vacant block and hide there for a while.

I did as she told me to, but missed jumping into the vacant block of land and landed on the next-door well-netted fowl yard. The fowls started to make a terrible racket, with the help of the old rooster. There I was, a girl of eighteen, in an undignified position on the sagging, dented roof of the fowl house. The worst then happened: the owner came out to see what the commotion was all about—and, oh, wasn't he real mad with me! I was conscious of the detectives next door. He roared at me and asked me what the devil did I think I was doing. Then, when I could get my faculties together, I said the first thing that came into my mind: a lie. I told him that I was sorry and that I was after a ball I threw over accidentally onto his fowl house. If he could please help me off, and give me some nails and [a] hammer, I would fix up his wire netting. I was sure I could do it.

He was a kind man and grudgingly heaped coals of fire on my head by saying, 'never mind' as he gave me his hand to pull me off the netting, 'look and see if your ball is around, and I'll fix the fowl netting'. As he went to get hammer and nails, I got through a little square hole in his brick fence. As I fell into the high grass on the other side, I could not help thinking, 'Oh Lord, I am sorry. This is what comes when I get mixed up in wrong things'. I lay in the grass as long as I could, then without being conspicuous, I got up and pretended to look out for a lost ball for the benefit that kind man. For a quarter of an hour, I pretended to search, then I climbed up and looked over Mrs Adams's fence to see if all was clear. She was in the yard doing something; she spotted me and told me 'to put my bloody head down', which I hurriedly did. Then I walked around looking for the imaginary ball, wishing I was safely back at Mrs Pierce's in Mosman with those children, especially that little baby.

My thoughts ran to the first little ones I used to mind—then Mrs Adams stuck her head up on the other side of the wall and hissed, rather than called, 'Come quick, get over here', which I did. I was deeply grateful to her and wonderful little dark Carrie. She did not know me much and could have washed her hands of the whole affair. They took me inside and looked around for clothes to disguise me. They gave me a long black skirt, I think it was Mrs A's, and to top it off, a black hat and veil. My gosh, I wondered why this had happened to me, and where was my sister May? I asked Carrie, and she said, 'she'll turn up and I'll tell her where you are'. Meanwhile, they were trying to find a job for me. They were told to try a warehouse on the corner in Cleveland Street, in Redfern. They were a family of Syrians. The old mother and father were dears, and hard-working. They had about seven children, three were grown up and one was married. I shared a bedroom with a girl of sixteen years. I was quite happy with them, they had dark skins, the routine was real haphazard. I just pleased myself where I cleaned up and how I did it. But they were pleased, and I really did my best. Then, somehow, I fitted in with the family so much that I didn't even get paid! The oldest daughter, Theresa, aged sixteen, was a dear. I'd go to their Syrian church. I got very fond of the whole family and their Syrian friends. Some didn't know how to take me; one of the oldest boys, three or four years older than me, asked me would I go to the pictures with him. He was a nice-looking young man, but I wasn't happy about going out with any boys just then. I wanted to feel free, but he wanted a 'yes' or 'no'. So, I reluctantly said 'yes'. He was a kind young man, but I was afraid of men.

Some weeks went by and I felt a longing to see Carrie and to hear if my sister May was about. Everyone but Carrie treated me very coldly.

I guessed they didn't wish to be mixed up with a runaway who the police were looking for. I felt that they were genuinely afraid.

Although I was somewhat settled with this Syrian family, I was restless all the same. I felt that I let down Miss Lowe of the Aborigines Protection Board. She had been good to me. We Aboriginal girls who were far away from home thought people were great if they just gave us a smile and said hello. Anyway, one Syrian young man, one of the family, liked me—the wrong way or the right way? I was a bit timid and I felt it wouldn't be the right way.

It's queer when I think of it now, but I phoned Miss Lowe after some weeks. She was the only one on the Aboriginal Protection Board I had confidence in. When I heard her voice on the phone answering me, I was full of fright, but stood my ground and told her who was speaking. She couldn't believe it, after months of not knowing where I was. She asked me to come in the next day to see her, which I did, taking Theresa, the Syrian girl, with me. She begged for me to be left behind with her family. However, I was sent to a sheep station twenty-five miles from Walgett and spent three years there.

Chapter Eleven

I did enjoy the train journey to Walgett. My third new mistress had a little girl about ten years old, a dignified, quiet little person with glorious long golden hair. They travelled in first class; I was quite happy in second class, with a middle-aged lady and her husband, and a couple of cheerful shearers. They started to sing softly, then they asked me if I knew any songs. I said 'yes' politely. As children we were never shy of singing; Mother taught us to sing in harmony and the missionaries taught us Sunday school choruses. I sang some Negro spirituals and some popular songs. Theresa, my Syrian friend back in Sydney, played the piano and used to buy all the latest songs. I would learn them with her.

They asked me to sing one after another. I enjoyed singing and the other gentleman and his wife asked me to sing different songs, if I knew them. It broke the boredom of the journey for all of us, and they all joined in too. I just sang and sang. My new mistress's little girl told me some weeks later, when she got to know me, that they heard me singing a couple of carriages back. I just thought, 'Oh my goodness!'

The drive to the sheep station was twenty miles from Walgett, further on about fifty miles was Brewarrina. I settled down and took delight in learning plain cooking. I loved to put all my energy into scrubbing the huge verandah around that lovely homestead, keeping it spotless. I liked this new mistress. She was older than the others and had a dry sense of humour, like her husband who was of Scottish origin. He was middle-aged. I liked and respected him at once—a man of very few words.

It was hard work in the busy season on that station. I would have some extra workmen to cook for, including an Aboriginal man, who said Mr Campbell was a very good boss. Then, who should turn up in one of the busy seasons, but the two friends who had asked me to sing on the train! I was glad to see them, they were cheerful and kind, and wanted to know how I was getting on.

The cooking, as I said, was easy because when they killed a sheep, once a week (or twice a week, if it was a cool season) we would have fresh meat for about three days. The rest would be salted down. The salted meat was very enjoyable too. There were no fridges in those days, only what you call a 'Coolgardie safe'. They were homemade with thin hessian around a frame. A square tin holding water was placed on top, and clean thick towelling, which was placed in the water, hung down the sides from the top. The water dripped constantly through this towelling. The safe was kept in a corner on the verandah where the breeze would blow through. It was remarkably effective for keeping butter, milk and fresh foods on the hottest days.

My mistress and boss had four children. The eldest girl and the two boys were away at college. I got on well with the boys and the youngest girl. I learned to ride a pony that the youngest girl used to ride everywhere. It wasn't happy till I learned to ride it properly. The little black thing didn't like me on its back. I think it knew I was scared.

It used to swell out its side by breathing out when I put the saddle on, and when I put my foot in the stirrups to get on its back, the little monkey would breath in; believe it or not! When I got on its back, the saddle would slip—slip—slip and I would find myself underneath its tummy. This would create a great deal of amusement if anyone was around, until someone told me that giving it a couple of good smacks on the tummy would counter this mischief. But this little fellow knew plenty more tricks. Once, when I found myself thrown off its back and sliding along the ground, I heard great laughter coming from the station hands, and looking around to see where my little friend the pony was, I was almost sure I could see a smile of glee on its face too!

Another experience was with my sister May. I was delighted to have her nearby, working on a neighbouring station about six miles away, for friends of the station owners that I was working for. My sister was a good rider, and she would ride over sometimes to see me. So, one day when she visited, I asked my boss, mistress and the little girl if I could go for a little ride on the pony. I was given permission, but told on no account to attempt to ride the big bay horse my sister was riding. I didn't relish being told that I couldn't ride well in this round-about way. So, when we were well out of sight of the station, I begged my sister to exchange horses. She was very reluctant and said that something might make me fall off. After she said that, I was more determined to ride it. I felt it was great sitting on that big bay, and my sister thought the pony was lovely. He started to trot, and then both horses went into a canter, then a gallop. I felt I had better pull my horse in, as there was a gate up ahead. I yelled to my sister to pull up, but she was in high glee and yelled with joy because the little pony was keeping up and holding its own with the big horse.

I could see the gate coming nearer and I was getting fearful. I felt so sure that my horse would stop abruptly at the gate and that I would go over it. I pulled at the reins, but the big horse was still going strong; I couldn't make him respond. Then he showed me how strong he was by kicking up his hindquarters. I do not remember my fall, but I think it was pretty spectacular because I found myself facing the opposite way to where I was galloping. What's more, I fell into a dusty big depression in the ground, made dry for want of rain. I came to and found my sister half-crying and calling to me. When she found I was 'in the land of the living' she was cross with the poor horse. Anyway, I got back on the little pony and my sister remounted her big horse, which was now quite docile.

The next morning, I could hardly move. I felt as though all my bones were broken. The mistress's brother, who would always come in early of a morning to have a cup of tea, then exercise the racehorses he was training, said to me, 'My word, you must have been going some on that horse, did you come a cropper?' I was amazed that this white man had tracked us down, so I owned up to what had happened. He laughed and laughed. I begged him not to tell, but I think he must have because I was not allowed to go riding for a while, but my sister would still come over to see me.

One day she came to stay for a week. Her boss and his wife had gone for a visit and I asked if she could come to stay with me.

We had great fun. One day (wash day) I was taking the washing off the line, which was very long, outside the kitchen gate. As I put the clothes in the basket I would go and get another armful. I looked back at the half-filled basket of clean washing to see two of our pet pigs, one half-grown and the other nearly full-grown, having the fun of their lives rolling in the lovely white sheets and tablecloths that I had washed. These pigs used to follow me everywhere and were such pets. However, as I ran to rescue my clean washing, my arms full with clothes, I screamed at them with rage. The rascals turned tail and fled. My sister's merriment knew no bounds. But she said, 'never mind, I'll help you wash them again'.

What with chasing and scolding young pigs who were rolling in my basket of washing, and other half-a-dozen piglets that I looked after who wouldn't let me out of their sight, it was very embarrassing! Sometimes I would have to hold fencing wire down the so that they could get through as I went to the mailbox half a mile away.

Then sometimes I had to lead or shoo the racehorses out of the fowl run, where they got in and robbed the chooks of their pollards. I also had to 'shoo' the half-grown sheep dog, whose instinct was to drive the fowls around like sheep, much to the fowls' disgust, until I rescued them.

Old Grace, the tabby cat, would break my heart. She was always having kittens and they would have to be drowned. One of her kittens which was lucky not to be drowned, young Katherine the boss's daughter called it 'Sticky Beak' because it wasn't afraid of anything. It would sneak up on the horses feeding just outside the kitchen fence, and when they got near him, he would just roll over and the horses would sniff him or nuzzle him and then they just kept feeding.

My sister and I enjoyed exchanging stories of our different experiences. We would go down to the bottom of the garden where the Chinese gardener would give us lovely blood-red watermelons when in season. There was plenty of fruit, and the lovely Barwon River flowed so swift there.

May worked for Mr and Mrs Burns, the managers at the little Aboriginal settlement a few miles out of Brewarrina. One day, during May's holiday and while my mistress and Katherine were away in Sydney, we were looking through May's case. She was showing me some things she prized very much and giving me one or two things: a pretty postcard or a handkerchief. We had a few delightful moments reading some of her letters from home; one from dear old Aunty inquiring how her 'ugly duckling' was getting on; meaning me! I knew she loved me very much and looked upon the name as a pet name. I didn't have any illusions about my looks or tickets on myself. My curly hair hung to my shoulders or was done up in an ungainly bun, and I was on the plump side. There was plenty to eat, plenty of work, a good bed, plenty of fresh air and mostly good common sense on that station. However, as I looked through May's things, my eyes picked out something else in her case. It was sinister-looking enough to me: a revolver. I could never stand the look of a rifle or one of those double-barrelled guns. Pointing at it, I gasped, 'Where did you get this from?' She hesitated, but then said that it belonged to the police officer in Wellington, where she had worked before she was sent to Brewarrina. His wife was hard to get on with, and was telling tales to her husband, the policeman. May was only sixteen then, and not a very strong girl. Once, they locked her up in the town gaol.

Another time, the policeman got so exasperated with the tales his wife told him that he hit May across the shins with a broom handle that was handy. This made her limp and cry for days with the pain. I was horror-struck as my sister told me her story. She finished by saying she came across this little revolver and, still sick with humiliation and pain, she carried it about with her. She said if he had hit her again, she was going to shoot herself. I prayed silently, thanking God she was safely there with me; but so was that horrible ugly little gun. When I asked her what on earth she was doing with it now, she said that she had fun with it, trying to shoot rabbits and wild ducks on the river. Sensing that I was troubled about it, however, she put the thing back in her case and closed it. Then she did me a favour by saddling the little pony and rounding up the cows and putting them in their yards to be milked in the morning. While she was away, I was drawn to that case of hers like magic. I opened it and gingerly took out the ugly little weapon. Then I hid it. When she packed all her things, as she was leaving to work on the neighbouring station, I held my breath, wondering if she would miss the gun. She did, and was very concerned, asking me did I take it and what I did with it. Half-crying, I blurted out that I did take it, and threw it in the river because I thought she might kill herself with it. She was quite hurt and said, 'You shouldn't have done that'. However, she forgave me after a while.

I still had it hidden and waited for a favourable time to throw it in the river. Meanwhile, young Katherine and the mistress came home from Sydney after their holiday. Katherine, though only thirteen, had grown very close to me, she was one of the greatest little girls that I ever knew. Anyway, I told her all about the gun. As a matter of fact, I showed it to her and put it back in my locker. That was the last I saw of it. Katherine must have told her parents and they rightfully confiscated it. I was thankful and fearful, but that was the end of it, and I did not hear any more about the gun.

I had turned twenty-one, and my sister was about nineteen-and-a-half. Life still went on, we learned to live with what we had to do. I even stopped dreaming of the time when I would see the old people again. I had dreams of marriage. I saw a few nice white young men, whom I admired from a distance, but never spoke to. I guess they did not even notice that I existed. I was shy of them all, even the young policeman whose duty it was to ride out once a month to see if we were getting on all right. I would get self-conscious when Mr Maskey, the mistress's younger brother, who was about twenty-six, would say 'Here's your friend coming to see you'. So, when the poor young constable would question me and ask me if I was all right, I would clam up and wouldn't answer him. He was embarrassed as well. He came all that distance and never spoke to me, but noted, apparently, that I was OK.

I do not know how long my sister and I would have been away from our people, but one day during the busy season, the boss's wife was very concerned. Her husband had gone out without his lunch; he left it on the table, and he had a long ride out [to] the back paddock where they were rounding up sheep. I very quickly asked if I could ride the pony to take the lunch out. My mistress hesitated, knowing all the falls I had had, so I eagerly promised that I would be careful. Katherine helped me put the bridle and saddle on, little knowing that it would be the last ride I would have on her little pony. I rode happily into the bush, following instructions and leaving all the washing up behind! I seemed a long long way, but the little pony was a real pet and for the first time I didn't fall off her. I found the boss. He was surprised, but pleased with having his lunch brought to him. He had a bit of a grin on his face as I cantered away home again. But, ugh, I remembered the washing up was waiting for me, and I remembered that I had to wash the separator as well! It was out in another part of the house and as I went around to do it, I saw a huge snake crawling up the side of the bench. He was after the drippings of cream and milk. Remembering the tiger snake that bit my sister, I gave a yell, 'Snake!' The mistress was there in a second, but it crawled under the house, especially close to the part where my room was. I was terrified. Every time I saw a shadow, I thought it was the snake.

Anyway, one day I was standing on the verandah discussing something with Katherine. Her mother was laughing at the antics of old Gracie, the mother cat. She was jumping around, her paws working overtime. Then we saw she was fighting with a snake. A shiver went right through me. I wasn't very brave where snakes were concerned. Young Katherine gave a cry for the old cat and rushed to its rescue. On principle, I was rushing with her, but the mistress stopped us and quickly picked up a garden spade. Just as quickly she said, 'Hold him, Gracie'. To my amazement, the old cat held it firmly near its neck while its tail was thrashing the air. Mrs Campbell calmly cut its head off; anyway, she made a mess of it. The old cat walked away with such graces, as much as to say, 'I could have made a better job of it'. Then we wondered where old Tom was, the father of most of the cats.

He had been missing for a week. He was a favourite with everyone. He often went hunting and when he arrived home, he had to have his wounds treated. We never knew what he was fighting with; maybe a goanna or a dingo he had been too slow to escape from. When some days had passed without seeing him, Katherine, whose pet he was, got very upset and we tried to console her. A little later we were walking down to the vegetable garden to get vegetables from the Chinese gardener, the mistress coming along too. I just happened to see a little bit of fur blowing with the wind, and we all rushed to it because the fur belonged to old Tom the cat. He was on his last legs. Flies were all around his mouth, and I told Katherine to keep back. We thought he was dead, but his tail was moving slightly. There were maggots all around his mouth. I had great admiration for that mistress, she prized that cat's mouth open and dragged out an ugly piece of bone that was stuck across the roof of his mouth. He was slowly starving to death. I remembered then, a few days before, how old Tom was trying to tell us, meowing piteously and rubbing against us. A few days of nursing and he was his old self again.

When the floodwaters came, I had to dive in the river to help the boss's teenage sons clear debris that got caught in the pipes that pumped water to the garden and up to the house for the shower and bathing purposes. (There was plenty of tank water for drinking and cooking). It was embarrassing at first, I was pretty shy, until I found it was an everyday occurrence and no one took any notice.

Chapter Eleven

I will never forget the week when everyone went down with the flu, one by one. The boss sent for his sister, who was a doctor. In the middle of it, I got the germ. Oh, my goodness, it frightened me when I coughed up blood and could hardly breath. (I can remember it quite well, because I have been very familiar with that type of cold, especially when I am exhausted; I catch it easily.) I was worried and thought, 'Oh no, I can't go to bed'. Everyone else was in bed except the boss, the doctor and me. So, I 'cracked hardy' as the old saying goes; when you pretend to be tough. I guess a lot of folks know that feeling. I was scared at times, because when I did too much I started coughing and could not breathe. My word, that's when I wanted my mother and the old folks at home. The lady doctor gave me medicine, but those verandahs had to be scrubbed, the milk separated from the cream, the meals had to go on, especially meals that were suitable for each sick one. The doctor was tired. I made her cups and cups of tea and we had some together. Well, everyone got better. I thanked God, I was so surprised to find myself alive and on my feet. I beamed when the boss said to me, 'Thank you, girl, you did well'. That was all I wanted.

Chapter Twelve

One day in the middle of the busy season, word came from the headquarters of the Aborigines Protection Board that May and I had to go home at once. The old uncle, Osley Ingram, was very ill and not expected to live. His dying wish was to see May and I before he passed on. The joy of going home was marred by the thought that we might not get home in time. We packed our few belongings; what I could fit in my one-and-only case. I also packed some big cardboard boxes. I found that May had done the same. May's boss drove her from his place, and my boss drove me the twenty-five miles to Walgett railway station. It was a long and tiring train journey, but we were going home; not to dear old Moonahcullah Aboriginal settlement on the Edward River, but to Barham township. A few of our people had moved to Barham township, so as to make a fresh start in a white town; to give their children an education and what they thought was a better way of life, the white way.

One of my cousins came to Koondrook railway station to drive us in the sulky to Uncle and Aunt's. Being away so long, the first thing my cousin, aged nineteen, said to me was 'What a funny hat you've got on. How long have you had it?' I felt horrified, as I had only just bought it and thought it was a very pretty one. Needless to say, my sister and I soon discovered how old-fashioned we were dressed.

We arrived at the old tiny shanty home, made from material they got from the tip. What was so refreshing was the garden of flowers blooming (Aborigines love flowers) and the vegetable patch on the little plot of land that they were trying to buy on the outskirts of Barham.

Our uncle was conscious for about an hour after we arrived, then he passed away. It was a big funeral. Flowers were plentiful on his coffin: wildflowers, gum leaves and garden flowers. He was buried in the Barham cemetery, in the whereabouts of his own tribal grounds. White people laughed at his pack of rabbit dogs as they followed the buggies to the cemetery. That was just on fifty years ago. The old aunt, Ethel, my mother's sister, died in the Deniliquin hospital eighteen years later, a lonely, uncared-for old lady. I didn't even know that she was ill; but I should have. I feel very guilty and my heart still aches because I only found out a week after she died. She was buried in a lonely grave in Deniliquin. I heard the details through an Aboriginal friend that I happened to meet later and mourned for my neglect. But I feel that she is at peace, because she was a good person. She and old Uncle helped multitudes, both dark and white. I can remember how she would not listen to any scandal. Old Aunt was like the three wise monkeys who 'saw no evil, heard no evil and spoke no evil'.

Let's face it—we have experienced real misery and painful outrage trying to belong in our own country, Australia, because some of our forefathers were white; causing us part-Aborigines to be divided from our kith and kin. I have seen this happen in a New South Wales training home, where Aboriginal girls were trained to be domestics; in other words, to be servant girls to any white 'mistress' or 'master'. Our boys were used the same way, for a very small wage. I never did know for sure what we were paid. I believe it was half-a-crown (or 50c) per week and 6d a week pocket money; the next year increasing to 1/– a week and 11–12d pocket money, and so on. It stopped for me, after I was there for twelve months. The half-crown was put in the bank by the government. I got just on 70 or 80 pounds for the nine years away; and believe me, I have heard from others how hard they worked.

After the old uncle was buried, May and I fitted in again with our people, as a matter of course, with their sufferings and joys. I will never forget those first few months home with my people—cold rainy weather, draughty homes made from materials from the tip, lined with hessian and papered over to seal the walls. Everyone got sick, mostly the flu. Sometimes we would be lucky to have one of our menfolk to cut and roll a huge log to fit in the back of our big fireplace, which would burn for days. Sometimes it would be too hot, and a door or window would be opened to let the cold air in. The colds and influenza would be numerous, that was when Old Man Weed, a plant growing close to the ground, was used. I mentioned before that it cures so much amongst my people and is getting known amongst the white people for the relief it gives. Goanna fat, or fat and a little mustard, is also good for colds when rubbed over the chest and between the shoulders. However, goanna fat was hard to get, living in the township of Barham, or any town then. White people's medicine was hard to get because there was no money to pay for it. I cannot remember there being a public hospital nearer than Deniliquin.

My mother had been constantly helping my aunt to care for old Uncle, both sitting up night and day with him. Many of our old and young people helped in this way too; this was our custom when we knew the end was near. Mother was not quite so young then. She was exhausted and really needed a rest, but she still went to work at some of the homes in town. May and I got temporary jobs to tide us over those hard times.

I have already told the story of our grandfather, George Middleton, whose farm had been sold out. He bought a small place in Moama on the New South Wales side of the Murray River. He felt that he needed the care of his daughters in Barham, which fell on my mother's shoulders, with old Aunt helping as much as she could. His wish was to be buried at Cummeragunja, near his wife and family. He passed away peacefully at Barham township, aged between eighty and ninety. Our older generation was not registered as babies, but as I have already said,

Grandfather was. He was one of three light-skinned babies born in a tribe that objected to that sort of thing happening. Their mothers kept a watchful eye on these babies till they were about three, as they could have mysteriously disappeared. However, I know when Grandfather died, his white relations, whom I have reason to believe had been in touch with Grandfather and his life's progress, asked that my mother and aunts spend a holiday at their home. Coming from the proud Ulupna tribe, while very touched and pleased, they declined the invitation. Mother and Aunt didn't even discuss it with us their children till years later, then not enough for us to find out who the white relations were. Perhaps it was better so, who knows?

We, the remnants of that tribe are still very proud, but I have learned to be humble and to try and love and care for all people, no matter what race or creed. It is very hard to keep calm and peaceful when I see the plight of my people and the misunderstandings and divisions where once there was real dignity and humbleness. Perhaps that is a thing of the past, but I believe that unity will come when Black and white work for it and fight for it together, loving and caring for each other. Again and again I repeat: colour is not the issue.

I liked Barham. The names Barham, Koondrook, Kerang and other names were familiar to me, and tales of Kow Swamp and other places where Uncle Osley and Billy Ingram and other relations' tribes have been buried for thousands of years.

Old Uncle Billy carried on as head of traditional tribal rights and relations after old Uncle died. I've seen this stately and elderly old man, who was slow to anger, tell a white man who dug up remains of our people that 'If he so much as put his feet on that sacred ground again he would not live to be sorry'. It is fresh in my memory as though it was yesterday. I know as time goes on, more remains of our people will be found all along the Murray River, Edward River, the Wakool and Murrumbidgee River. I feel strongly that these old burial grounds should not be disturbed. Let's face it, even the educated Aboriginal youth of today do not know the history of our people and often question the

Billy Ingram and his brother Jack (in the boat), brothers of Margaret's uncle Osley Ingram.

truth of stories handed down. Very few elderly Aboriginal people who are living have these stories, the treasured truths. Here in Victoria and New South Wales, our Aboriginal people are more together now than they have ever been, and those that do not know about tribal happenings of long ago are eager to learn.

When irresponsible ones use liquor to make 'Dutch courage', it fosters a wider gap of misunderstanding and makes Aborigines look like a race of no-hopers all over the world, wherever news carries. Only a handful of irresponsible Aborigines act like this. God only knows the answer to their frustration and bitterness. My people, whom I love, are an asset to this country. Our problems did not get like this overnight. Human nature is the same the world over. Colour is not the issue. The answer is there for all to see; not *who* is right, but *what* is right.

I am thrilled at the knowledge handed down about our people. It is as though the old people are trying to relay a message, not only to their race, but to the human race. Do we flatter ourselves that we are better off today than they were—maybe in a few material goods, but what peace of mind have we got? We will never know [the] peace of mind and heart they had, but let's live in truth and honesty. Never mind how the other person is wrong, let's start with ourselves and care for the one who doesn't care for themselves or anyone else. I make many mistakes and believe me it's hard to have courage to right some of these mistakes. I pray that with God's help I can fight for what is right, and to fight that old snake of hate and bitterness when it rears its head. Don't let us lose the dignity and love our old people had for all people. They shared what they had with any humans, white or dark, in kindliness.

Chapter Thirteen

Quite a lot of our young Aboriginal girls found it difficult to get work in the country, so they drifted to Melbourne. A few had relations living there, and they acted as stepping stones, letting the young ones stay with them until they found jobs. Although these families were struggling, they shared what they had. Two families that I remember when I first came to Melbourne were our old schoolteacher Mr James and family, and dear old Aunty Grace Bux, the mother of Dolly and Edgar Bux whom I went to school with at Cummeragunja. She would try to let out rooms in those hard times, poor old dear, but she would hardly ever get tenants that paid; until they got a job. I was one of them. My second youngest sister Evelyn was boarding with Aunty Grace and her family as well. She was nearly eighteen and offered to help pay my board until I got a job. It was generous of her, as she did not get much. She was just a factory worker, and fifty years ago the pay was not much. Aunty Grace's son was married to a lovely white lass and they had two children. He had a beautiful voice and was well known for singing in hotels, with the collection for that day going to the Children's Hospital. He was in his seventies when he died. He was crippled then but got about in his wheelchair and sang to the end. His wife, Lill, looked after him. Well, to get back to Chapel Street, South Melbourne, where I first stayed in Melbourne …

Chapter Thirteen

After working three years on Burumbil station I was still a bit cagey about meeting people, especially of the opposite sex. I was conscious of the fact that I was a bit old-fashioned, a country bumpkin as the old saying goes. But I had three proposals of marriage in Barham: from two very nice Aboriginal men, good workers, and one white man. He was very nice too. Only thing, the white man was shorter than I was. I guess I wasn't ready for romance in any colour or form. Still, I can remember I had two proposals of marriage at Cummeragunja during a short stay there. If I had accepted, I would have been Sir Douglas Nicholls first cousin-in-law. They were great fellows, and both had big families. Their wives were pretty girls and great friends of mine. I felt a bit of a coward.

Before I left Barham, my mother was midwife to a young Aboriginal woman who was having her first baby. A custom of ours was to visit the baby immediately after birth. The baby was only about half an hour old, dear little cuddly fellow, lying in his proud mummy's arms. Then Mother, who was in the midst of cleaning up after the birth, called we four daughters, 'Margaret, May, Evelyn and Geraldine, come here. I wish you to see this and learn'. We were curious to see what she wanted to show us. I do not think that my two younger sisters or even May showed their feelings. The younger ones would have helped Mother on one or two occasions, but I was a bit shocked as Mum explained everything—the afterbirth and so forth. I stayed as long as I felt I should, then I bolted for home. After that I couldn't think of marriage without shuddering secretly.

One nice Aboriginal man pursued me the few days I was at Cummeragunja. I made sure that I was always with a group of people, so that he couldn't get me on my own. Bless him, he was a determined person and sent a note over to where I was staying, saying his mother would like to meet me before I left for Melbourne. I coaxed, bribed and begged two girl friends to accompany me and not to leave me alone with him. So, with misgivings, I went to his home. It was nicely kept, and his mother was a stately, gracious woman. I liked her instantly and felt proud to know her. Somehow, I found myself alone with her tall, good-looking son and I panicked for a few moments. But he was kind and nice, and simply asked me to marry him. I wasn't afraid of him anymore. I liked him very much, but only knowing him a few days, I told him that I would write to him and get to know each other. I did make an attempt to get to know him, but trying to find a job and other things, I let off writing to him.

My first trip to Melbourne I liked very much—Great Depression and all! I walked my shoe leather off looking for jobs. Although I walked for miles, I felt free. Everything was a challenge and, in a sense, I became obsessed with trying for jobs. I walked to St Kilda one day, miles further than I should, because I did not know the way. I always asked ladies to direct me. After a couple of weeks (this was in the 1930s) I answered an advertisement for a nurse girl to two small children. A pretty young lady came to the door and I got the job.

The children were two boys, aged two and four. The job was so easy, and they were charming business-people, very modern. I didn't feel like a servant. I went for car rides with her and the family for picnics. I was still terribly shy with the opposite sex, and my tongue would go muddled when her husband would try to talk with me. He was very kind, sincere and sophisticated. I learned a lot from this young 'mistress', who was very charming, gay, and I thought beautiful. She was a lovely singer. We were more like real friends, she trusted me.

Sometimes in the middle of my work, she would say, 'Please take the children to the park or down the beach', which wasn't far away, because she wanted quiet to do some writing or something. She would usher me out, saying that she would finish the work. Working for that family was one happy time. They asked me if I would like to have my meals with them, or with the two little boys. I said that I would like to have it with the two little boys. I believe that when the boys were grown-up, they excelled themselves in high ranks of the army during the last world war. However, like all children I was nurse girl to, I grew fond of them and know they liked me. I also enjoyed the walks. I used to take them down on the beach (Elwood) or into the parks.

Chapter Thirteen

On my days off, the only place I knew to visit was Aunty Gracie's. She was gay and had a nice-looking daughter, Dolly, who we went to school with. Dolly was, I felt, like a sister to me. Aunty Gracie's eldest son was killed in the First World War.

Anyway, I loved to talk with Aunty Grace and Scottie, as they called her husband. However, Dolly asked me would I like to go to a party with her. Before I could answer, my younger sister said, 'No, Doll, leave her, she will want to go home early'. I felt indignant and said—against my better judgement—that I would love to go with her. Dolly did my hair and face up. I secretly rubbed the muck off before I got to the party. It was my first in Melbourne, but not the last for quite a while! It was a well-conducted party and I was introduced to everyone. Trays of drinks were carried around by the hostess, who praised me when I said, 'No, thank you' and she got me a soft drink. Then [a] young man came in and everyone greeted him. He was a dapper little fellow, but I didn't take much notice of him or any of the menfolk. They were all enjoying themselves. I loved looking and admiring the ladies' pretty dresses. Dolly and I were introduced. We talked, at least Dolly did: I was mostly dumb. This young man was called Squizzy. He said, 'Hello', but I was just looking and taking everything in. When I got home, Dolly got to telling everyone we went to this swell party that Squizzy Taylor was at. My sister looked shocked, 'Oh no, you didn't take Margaret to there?'

'Of course, I did; you all went out and left her.'

Anyway, I asked why they were all shocked about this Squizzy Taylor, who was he? They told me he was a wanted gunman. After I got over my shock, I said, 'He seemed nice and I didn't see any guns'. After hearing a few more stories about him, it was my first and last party for a long time.

When I first started to meet people, the right kind and the wrong kind, I liked them all as friends. I was slowly getting used to people, both sexes, and they treated me with respect. I went home now and again to see the old aunt and Mother, who was still usually visiting

Cummeragunja, her home settlement. Old Aunt occasionally went out to Tulla station, rabbiting with her pack of dogs. She did not and would not eat rabbit, no matter how hungry she was, but she sold the rabbit skins to keep her in food and to feed her dogs. Too much rabbit wasn't good for the dogs; they would get thin and waste away if they did not have a varied diet. So, the old aunt would harness up the horse to the four-wheel buggy; sometimes May and I would go with her. It was amazing how she would—old as she was—spot the squatting rabbits from where she was sitting in the buggy. She was such a straight shot with her rifle. More often than not, she would get them through the head, killing them instantly. The old Aboriginal people didn't get government rations or pensions then. How they lived and died was nobody's business. It makes me feel quite ill with remorse; how I could have helped those beloved old people more, especially lonely old Aunt, who didn't complain or asked for anything.

I feel quite miserable and my heart aches when I think how selfish young people can be, some without knowing it. What brings this home to me is when I remember once, when I was working, I was getting 22 shillings a week in Melbourne. I had the thought to send 10/– home to the dear old lady, and promptly came back a letter to say, 'God bless you, my girl. Thank you'. She went on to say how she was so hungry and hadn't food in the house to speak of when she got my letter with ten shillings in it. She went down [to] town and bought sausages, tea, sugar, vegetables and bones for the soup and for her two little dogs she had left (her only company). She thanked me several times in the letter. I am far from young now, and I shed tears when I remember that instance, and wonder how many young folk selfishly and unthinkingly neglect their old ones, who did without, such as I. Money is necessary for sure, but love and care for all people, no matter what the colour or age, is more important. I feel a certain consolation that I will join her and my loved ones in spirit in this beloved country's earth that owns and cradles us when we are tired and have that long last sleep. In peace I will join all loved ones in the old camping ground of millions of years.

Margaret and her daughter Mollie.

It would make my story too long to tell of the struggles of young Aboriginal females in the cities. I felt the divisions between different colours and devoured books (the wrong kind, I know now) about views on Aborigines. I felt we were the least advanced of all coloured races. Even the coloured people from overseas would not mix with us in those days. I got to feeling discontented with my people's lot and wondered in my heart, 'What was the answer?' Were we Aborigines only meant to be used as servants for the white people? So, the thought came to me to marry a white man, so that my children would be light-skinned and they would have equal opportunities living as white children.

How ignorant I was! Yes, I was in love with an Aboriginal young man; I used to write to him when I worked in Sydney, but he got married to a nice Aboriginal girl. He has a grown-up family of lovely children now, in fact he is a grandfather, and we are all friends.

Well, I did marry a white man. He was in the navy. His family was very proud. I cannot tell of the heartaches I had in the first part of that marriage, because of my black skin. I accepted the home they gave me in Elwood. My husband had left the navy and couldn't find a suitable job, so we had to live with them. Those were Depression days. First, I lived in Barham with my little girl, aged fourteen months, who was still on the breast because we didn't have any food in the house for days at a time. My Aboriginal people scattered in Barham would tactfully share what little food they had with me, until I heard one little girl, home from school, asking her mother for a piece of bread. Her mother replied that there wasn't any and said she didn't know where the next lot was coming from. I was so shocked and ashamed. I had been eating the food their little children should have had. I quietly went home to old Aunty's shack. I cannot remember where she was then. I know my mother was in Sydney or Cowra or working.

However, I sat down once more and wrote to my husband, pleading with him to send some money for food for the baby. I did not realise that he was still out of work and his people were keeping him. His family were well-known pioneers of Tasmania who had recently moved to Melbourne. They were very upset that their son had married an unknown Aboriginal girl. Well, I was unfortunately not full-blooded, but brown-skinned.

I didn't get a letter from my husband, but from his sister, sending my fare to come to them straight away. I heard later that his sister was pressing my husband's suit for a job interview. She came across my letter in his pocket, telling of my baby and I starving. I don't think he meant to ignore us, but he was helpless to do anything for us and too afraid to ask his family. His sisters were very cross with him and his mother said I had to come to them. I did not realise the heartache and shame an Aboriginal girl could bring to a white family (some white families) by marrying their son. I did not know either the heartache or tears that would be shed when I realised what I had done in my ignorance of mixed marriages. Every time their friends came, I made myself scarce. They did not tell me to—I sensed it was better so—but I would cry my heart out. Served me right, I know. Out of three white men who asked me to marry them, why did I have to love the wrong one! Why didn't I marry one of my own people?

Anyway, they adored my little girl and I accepted them and fitted in with their relatives. Later, I got jobs. It tore my heart out to leave my little girl, but they were very good to her, especially Grandma and Grandpa. My father-in-law, who was a JP, in my opinion didn't worry about what colour I was from the first. He was very understanding and kind. My mother-in-law, whom I grew very fond of in spite of things, was very attached to my little girl. Gradually, to my secret delight and happy feelings, they started to introduce me to their people, saying, 'This is Marge'. But the old man, the father, would say, 'This is my daughter-in-law'. I did love the old people and grew fond of the whole family, and they of me. One day, the youngest brother was on the same bus with me. He was sitting right at the back. He was a shy boy of about nineteen years. I was sitting in the front. He told his mother how he watched all the white ladies looking at me. He felt, in his opinion, that they were staring at me and were not fit to wipe my shoes.

My feelings were sky high when I heard that—not because of what he said, but because he was shy and hardly held a conversation with me. It was like a little affection given to me from that family. However, they gradually accepted me.

On my mother-in-law's death bed, I realised how I had grown to love this family, and especially the old people who did keep their eyes on my little girl. I got her educated in a convent, paying for her. She was very upset when the old lady died. My mother-in-law told me, as I cried, her last words to me were, 'You are more of a lady than my son is a gentleman, and we love you for yourself'. I have treasured those words from a very proud old white lady because it made me feel it was worth trying to live without bitterness and hate in one's heart. I did love that old couple and, yes, their family in the end. First because they sincerely loved my little girl, and later I sensed their affection for me. I realised my motives for marrying a white man were wrong and that I, in my ignorance, had hurt this family too.

I drifted away from my husband, like many couples, after the war. He served almost from the first till the end of the Second World War with the Ninth Division and was one of the Tobruk Rats. I haven't seen him for almost twenty-six years. I know where he is. He is not in good health. My daughter visited him recently and he was pitifully glad to see her. I may go to see him one day, to show I have no ill feelings, least of all sentimental ones. I am sure he hasn't any either, after all these years. I think he has seen only one of his grandchildren, out of fourteen, nine great-grandchildren—beautiful even if I say so—and many adopted grandchildren, grandnephews and nieces. They love to visit me. I love them all and I am never lonely. But I am a little ahead of my story …

When the Second World War started, my mother-in-law and family and I had not seen their son, my husband, for two years. Then he came home in uniform.

My husband spent those last precious days of his final leave with me and our little girl, then aged twelve. She was very proud of him, and to be honest, I was too. Anyway, I'll not forget the parting, wondering

Back row from left: Barbara Burns, Mollie Burns (nee Tucker), Diane Singh (nee Day), Selwyn Burns (on knee), Alan Burns, Marcie Briggs. Front row from left: Rodney Burns, Maxine Barr (nee Burns), Alan Burns Jnr, Darryl Burns.

if we would ever see him again. With his arms around our little girl and I, we wept together—and for months after. Then we put our hearts into being patriotic, doing war work. I got work at Kinnear's Ropeworks in Footscray, a huge place. The boss, a very tall fair man, interviewed me and asked if I was Italian. I had long since lost my fear of men. I answered him and said, 'My goodness, they wouldn't be flattered, hearing you ask me that question. For one thing, they have nice noses, while mine is a flat Aboriginal nose. Besides, I feel they need work too. Some were born and bred here as well'. Well, Mr Kinnear kindly explained that the workers, being at war with Italy, would not work with them. I said that I was sorry, and my heart ached for them all. However, this kindly boss took me around the works, a huge place, and asked me what machine I would like to use. Oh my, my mind went blank. I had not used anything like these machines in my life! My pride wouldn't let him or any of the workers around (men) see that I was plumb scared. In my pride I chose a HUGE ninety-six-bobbin machine, with ninety-six strings running through it. I had to keep the strings from breaking on ninety-six other gadgets, without stopping the machine. I also had to keep water in the little gadgets that the string went through as the machine worked.

That water made it a bit damp and the cement floor a little slippery. A red-headed young man was my teacher. I asked him how long it would take to learn, and he said about three weeks. I thought, 'Oh my goodness'. However, he was a good teacher and I learned it all in a little less than three weeks. I loved that big powerful machine and working at Kinnear's rope factory. From the bosses down to all the workers, and there were hundreds of them, they were all my friends. My cousin Sally Russell and her son worked there as well, long before I did, so her friends were my friends.

The Christmas break-ups were something to remember. We would have a concert in the canteen and all good things to eat. Comedians came to entertain us. Two great singers, Max Reddy and Stella Lamond, were also asked to entertain. To my amazement and fright, I was asked to sing too! My workmates coaxing and bullying me when I said, 'Oh no, I don't have the courage'. Well, I did, I sang Silent Night in English and then in the Aranda Aboriginal language. They were all pretty merry and gave me a good clap, stamping the floor.

However, with the dampness of the work I was doing, I was easily catching too many colds, which were hard to get rid of, so regretfully I left. After I got well, I felt I should be patriotic and do something while the war was on. I was told that they wanted workers at the ammunition factory. I think when they saw that I was Aboriginal they hesitated, until they read the form that I had to fill in. It said that my husband was overseas in the war zone.

I liked working there; there was a lovely big canteen with a stage and music. But I shuddered at the bullets that were being made. I was on the machines. I liked working machines. On night shift, to stop going to sleep while we worked, we would start singing till the whole works were joining in. I couldn't help myself; I loved singing and would go for my life on the high notes.

Our forelady formed a committee to sing at the military hospital at Heidelberg. We loved doing that and would shed tears when we would go the next time and find an empty bed; where a friendly soldier had passed on. On one occasion we were passing a ward, when a young sick soldier standing at the door asked the head sister why we couldn't come in and sing to them. No-one visited them. So busybody-me asked the head sister, who said that they had TB. Anyone going into their ward had to be careful and went at their own risk. I thought to myself, 'Is that all?' I've lived on Aboriginal settlements where TB was constantly killing our people. I told the sister and begged her to let us visit them, and that we would be OK. We Aboriginal members of our concert party put it before all the rest, and everyone wanted to give back to those who had given so much for us. It was the gayest ward! They were hectic years indeed.

My husband was in Tobruk and then was sent to Papua New Guinea to clean up there and send the Japanese home. His praise for the Fuzzy Wuzzy Angels was so great. However, he got malaria; many of the soldiers came home with it. It was a nasty disease. I can remember him getting an attack of it. I phoned for an ambulance to take him to the repatriation hospital. While I stood by as he was being made comfortable, one of the ambulance nurses in khaki uniform said in a business-like way, looking at me, 'Who is this, she shouldn't be here'. I didn't answer her. Sick and all as my husband was, he was cross with her and snarled at her, 'She has every right to be here, she is my wife'. My heart went out to him as the ambulance took him away.

The war divided a lot of families: pitiful cases. The young men went away to war and those who came home again needed such care and love, only to find that wives didn't know how to respond to them. I feel it was pitiful. Many drifted apart, like we did. I, for one, am sorry for a lot of those shattered lives and marriages.

Chapter Fourteen

In 1933, my in-laws went to manage an orchard in the Hastings district. Grandpa was a very experienced orchardist and much in demand, although getting on in years. Mollie, my daughter, went to live with them when she was five years old, and went to school there, walking through the scrub. Even then, she would do her bit around the farm, milking the cows (and adding water to it if it didn't look enough—she admitted ashamedly when she was older!) and feeding the fowls. When she was older, we felt it would be better for her to go to a boarding school. Fortunately, a well-known convent in Abbotsford took her, which gave Mollie a great start in her education. Mollie loved the sisters in the convent during the seven years she was there. At weekends I would take her and several other white children for outings. During holidays she would stay with her grandfather and grandmother at Hastings, or with me, when I was with Mr Claude and Mrs Nora Smith. She loved music and learned to play the piano, violin and guitar, ukulele and autoharp, not brilliantly, but fairly well. She had a wonderful ear for music and perfect pitch.

I remember one instance when I was staying with my communist friends, who took me in when I did not have anywhere to stay. This was long before I met my Aborigine people in Fitzroy. I was very ignorant about anything in politics or any 'isms'. The only thing that stood me in good stead was what I was taught by my mother and old aunt; their strict discipline and loving kindliness. Plus, the missionaries—a lot of this teaching stuck to my inner being. I soon learned to use my singing voice and was much sought after for concerts and entertainment. It was wonderful fun for me, a young Aboriginal woman, who from childhood had watched my Aboriginal race grovel in the dirt, suffering indignities too miserable and too low to speak of. Little things, like putting my hand out to shake hands and only to be given a 'How do you do' in return.

While inwardly timid and quick to feel slights, I was popular at dances and concerts. People asked me to take part in entertainment evenings and parties in well-known high-society homes. I would always take my ukulele along, and I felt happy in any company singing, singing, singing! I would be sitting on the chair, and these high-society people—after having a few drinks—would be sitting around me on the lush carpets singing in their cultured voices. We sang such songs as *Way Down upon the Swanee River, Old Black Joe, Carry Me Back to Old Virginny, Sweet Genevieve* and others. Then I would hear them saying, 'She speaks beautiful English. She speaks better than we do!', and one lady snapping back, 'Speak for *yourself*'. When it ended, I would be driven back to the beautiful home where I was maid-of-all-works. Just as well, it brought me right down to earth and reality. I was just an Aboriginal maid, getting to love parties and all that they stood for: a so-called good time.

Then a white society lady called Helen Baillie found me and asked me to sing in a church concert in aid of our Aborigines in Fitzroy. That was the beginning of understanding and working for my people and others in the only way I knew. In the mid 1930s, I fitted in well doing social work with others of my people, fine well-known families such as the Lovetts and Clarkes of the Western District, and a little later with the Taylors. Jessie Taylor—who was a King from the Western District—was later a great contributor to our socials. She played piano accordion, and one of her daughters (who is like a daughter to me) played guitar and piano.

A portrait of Margaret in her concert attire.

We were doing our social work activities—all were for the betterment of our Aboriginal people—with the help of white people. Miss Helen Baillie was one of the genuine ones. She gave up her time, her home, and her life for Aboriginal people who then lived in Melbourne. I can honestly say she was the sincerest person. She did not expect honours or glory for it. Every person of the older generation in Fitzroy also remembered the good work of Mr Burdeu. Uncle Bill Cooper introduced me to the late Mr Claude Smith and his wife Mrs Nora Smith. I worked for them in their home, which was more like my own home. They did not lose patience with we Aborigines in those days: brushes with police mostly for drinking and brawls with whites (Fitzroy drunks) who, in greater numbers, called them a 'black nuisance'.

Mrs Smith helped me cut out and sew dresses and make hula skirts for our Aboriginal concerts, which we gave in aid of the Red Cross, kindergartens, schools and many other things. In those days it was nothing for Mr and Mrs Smith to have a large group to use their home for concert practice, or to have up to twenty Aborigines to a Sunday dinner: with roasts, vegetables and plum pudding. I cannot remember how that family of Smiths fitted them all in, to sit down around the table. All the men and women would help clear the table and wash up, and then we would all go around the piano in the sitting room. We sang a mixture of grand old hymns, songs and Aborigine songs that we would learn from each other in different dialects. We would have our guitars, ukeleles, mandolins, banjos and gum leaves. Oh, it was clean enjoyment! Mr Claude Smith would play the ukulele too. And those that could play the ukulele, but didn't own one, he would buy them one. His children were like our brothers as well, and his friends were our friends. This great family: pioneers of Footscray, a Justice of the Peace, estate agent, leader of many affairs, his wife a gentle personality but a great force in the home, gave my committee of women a piece of ground for a hostel. It was sold and the money used for Aboriginal needs. It didn't go far, but it encouraged we Aboriginal women to keep on, hoping and praying that our voices may be heard. We were trying to pull our weight, together with the white Aussies, in righting many wrongs and misunderstandings. As my old mum used to say, 'Stop feeling sorry for yourself and be up and doing'.

The first Aboriginal organisation that was formed in Victoria was the [Australian] Aborigines' League, of which I was the first treasurer. When I look back, I wonder where on earth I found the courage to take that on! However, it wasn't hard because we didn't have much money given to our fund.

Mr William Cooper's son, Lynch Cooper (of whom we Aborigines were very proud), won the World Sprint Championship somewhere in the 1927–1929 years. Many of our young Aboriginal men won 'gifts' in sport, including the late Selwyn Briggs, my sister Geraldine's husband. He was a cousin of Sir Douglas Nicholls. We all went to school together at Cummeragunja. Sir Douglas was also a gift winner and a famous footballer in the Fitzroy Football Club, along with Eddie Briggs and many others. We were delighted at the Cummeragunja football team being premiers seven years running. I feel a lot could be told about the sportsmanship of our Aboriginal menfolk and their struggles to live by high moral standards on those settlements managed by white men. The first lot of managers really tried to give their best, and our people responded. We had Aboriginal choirs, at Cummeragunja and Lake Tyers, trained by the same manager, Mr Bruce Ferguson, his wife and daughters.

An outstanding young man of his day was Jack Patten, one of six children and the brother of Bill Onus's first wife. He enlisted in the Second World War and went away with the second AIF to the Middle East. His love of humorous practical jokes got him into many scrapes in his regiment. On one occasion, he wanted leave to go and get a drink and smokes, which was out of bounds. He was refused, so he tried to slip out dressed as an Arab; but was caught by the Australian military police and run back into barracks.

Jack and his young brother were close friends, so much so that Jack's was George's and vice versa. At one point, George had quite a big roll of notes he wished to keep to himself, but knowing Jack, he realised he must hide it. Jack watched him like a hawk as they sat together on their beds. Thinking he would give George the opportunity to hide the roll under his bed or somewhere else Jack would find it easily, he said, 'I'll go outside for a bit of fresh air'.

They went to bed, and in the morning, Jack scratched his head and said, 'Where on earth did you hide that money?' George shouted with laughter and said, 'You get up, and I'll show you'. He lifted up Jack's own bed and there was a roll of notes. Jack had been sleeping on it all night!

Jack, like so many of my people, was initiated into drinking white people's liquor (grog) in order to drown his sorrows. Jack came through the war without a scratch but broke his leg on the ship as he travelled home. He was cared for in a military hospital in Sydney. Jack and his brother George did a lot of work for the Aboriginal cause in the early years (the 1930s) and from 1952–1957. Because of hard times, no work, they lived on sustenance and hand-outs, jumping trains to get around and interstate between Sydney and Melbourne. They did a lot to bring understanding of Aboriginals' plight to the public. They were two of the most daring Aborigines. I do not say that they were correct in their methods, but they caused a great stir, bringing forward the real plight of our people. They were gifted speakers and were much sought after by desirable and undesirable elements. George spent most of his time in Victoria, but Jack worked in both states.

Jack Patten had started school at Cummeragunja, but later went to school at Tumbarumba and Wyalong. His father, my mother's brother-in-law (also called Jack) was a police black tracker in Wyalong and that area. His children had a great opportunity of equal education in these town schools. Tales of his work as a black tracker were amusing. I never tired of hearing them: sheep stealing, cattle stealing and even murder out in the outback huts. He was very clever and valuable. Uncle Jack Patten did not talk about himself, but his white and dark friends loved telling these true stories of his powers of observation: getting to the root of the trouble.

On one occasion, Uncle went with the police to investigate the murder of a white woman and her son in a bush hut. Her other son told the police he had gone home and found them murdered. Uncle Jack found a bloodstained axe cunningly hidden in the bush. He went to a gum tree where he noticed recent axe marks. The jagged edge of the axe he'd found matched up with the marks in the tree and on wood left on the wood heap, which led him to believe the brother himself was the murderer. Further clever sleuthing proved this to be the case.

On another occasion, the police were called out to deal with cattle stealing. As usual, they took Uncle Jack. They found nothing, but persevered and went out again several times. One night they went to an outback cottage. While the police were snooping around outside, Uncle Jack went inside where he found a game of cards in progress on a long kitchen table. He sat down on the wooden bench that families used in those days. Uncle Jack noticed that the men were trying not to be fidgety and, as he watched, his hands were feeling underneath the table. He discovered there was a furry substance nailed underneath. Later the men were charged with stealing cattle and selling their skins to a gang of crooks.

Jack Patten Jnr won a scholarship and was put into the navy for training as a midshipman. He was fourteen, or about that age, at the time. He was homesick and ran away back home to his dusky family. I can remember how all of our families were disappointed, especially our grandfather, George Middleton.

Jack was married after some time and had a family, but he was always restless and worrying about his people's plight. Aborigines from different settlements would seek out Jack or write to him, pleading with him to come and help them and give them ideas about what to do. They were desperate days. A new generation of white managers was now in charge of the Aboriginal settlements. Some were very understanding and learned from the Aboriginal people. Others were arrogant and created favourites or encouraged tale carriers. That was brought home to me the time when I visited my sister, who was ill, and I went up to look after her.

I'll admit being ready to believe all that was said about this particular manager and his wife. He often, when speaking to the men, said, 'Come on, you black bastard'. I feel now, years later, that with real care we could have helped this manager and his wife to understand our people.

Jack Patten Jnr arrived at Cummeragunja after being sent for by the majority of Cummeragunja Aboriginal people. He was told to get off the settlement by the manager. The Aboriginal people made up their minds that if Jack was not allowed on Cummeragunja, they would not stay on either. So, sacrificing their dole or rations, the only food and livelihood in those depression days, and with babies, children and their sick people and elderly, they followed Jack across the Murray River to the state of Victoria. It was still the same land that belonged to us in our tribal days. We, the descendants of the Ulupna, Yorta Yorta, Wiradjuri and other tribes, with all our belongings, pitched camp at Barmah.

Then the hardships began: no milk for those babies or food rations. I have long felt that the two or three families that didn't leave Cummeragunja, as well as homesteaders around Barmah, must have helped with milk for those babies. My sister was still very sick, but she moved with the rest. They had to be resident in Victoria for three months before they could be put on the dole or sustenance, so there was a little sheep stealing and other little petty things. The police came out only to find nothing, and yet evidence was right under their noses. Maybe they were too kind-hearted. I like to think that. However, when Jack Patten led them over the Murray River to the Victorian side, the police were there from Moama, on the New South Wales side, to arrest him. But not before he gave my sick sister May a telegram to be sent to Sydney. I know now that it was addressed to a well-known publisher and book shop in Macquarie Street, Sydney. The result was that Jack Patten, whom the police had arrested and put in gaol, was out within half an hour of being put in; bail, I suppose, being sent.

Those of us in Melbourne walked our shoe leather off, cadging or begging for food for the protestors. I even went as far as to flirt with a taxi driver, begging him to cart food up to the Cummeragunja refugees.

We had meat from Angliss [Meatworks] in the city, some tins of food, some medicine and sugar. When we reached Mooroopna, this taxi driver was on our side and anxious to help in every way. He helped buy two big bags of flour, bags of sugar, fruit and whatnot—overloading his car. The people were very grateful for it. However, on the return journey to Melbourne, the good-hearted chap found his tyres all frayed. His car was in a bad way and it cost him a bit to repair. He turned out to be a sincere friend who treated Aboriginal females with respect.

Jack Patten and others in Sydney did what they could there. Many still refused to go back, sick and all, as most had colds or the flu. Some were forced to return to the settlement because of no food and no schooling for their little ones. Others travelled to Mooroopna and Shepparton. The hardships for such families as Selwyn Briggs and his family are an example. He and Geraldine got material from the rubbish dump to make a shelter in Daish's paddock in Mooroopna. I can remember my brother-in-law with his face tied up: a swollen gland and neuritis, struggling to make some sort of makeshift shelter. My sister, helping, was just skin and bone and sick too. I think they had four little children at the time. Others were in the same position, but they were all determined to make a go of things. Some felt they were not welcomed in the township.

When the fruit season began, there was work tomato picking, packing and canning—at which the Aboriginal women excelled. Most of our Aborigines from the Cummeragunja walk-off camped down near the banks of the Goulburn River. Oh, the hardships getting water up those steep banks. One old woman fell and broke her leg trying to get a billy can of water (so funny, but not so funny). She was cared for in the Mooroopna hospital. Years later, their children's children took part in fundraising efforts for this same hospital, where many of our old people were cared for and died, including my mother. My brother-in-law Selwyn, with his wife and children, are respected citizens of Mooroopna and Shepparton. They have their own home in a nice part of town, and other people have the same.

The descendants of the Patten family live here, there and everywhere. Uncle Jack Patten, I believe, was born in Healesville, Victoria, and married George Middleton's youngest daughter, Christina. They all had English names given by white people [in] those days. Aboriginal names were hard for white managers and schoolteachers to remember—such a pity. My Aborigine name, Lilardia—meaning a flowering plant—is pretty, but regarded a weed in gardens. Rather attractive, I think! The name was given to me by old Uncle William Cooper; father of Lynch Cooper, Sally Russell, the late Amy Charles, Jessie Mann and Gillian Cooper. Their late brother, Dan Cooper, was killed in the First World War. Min, Aunt Minnie, as all our people know her, is very gifted in education and can go far if helped in the right way. She is the only first cousin I have on my mother's side. I have a few on my father's side. His brother, Ernie Clements, was somewhere living in the Dubbo district and my father's youngest sister May's family; whom I long to see but have never met. My father's sister Ada married Pat Freeman: a very fine couple. Uncle Pat's people lived in Yass, New South Wales. His and Aunt Ada's granddaughter Margaret married a fine upright young Aboriginal (born in Victoria) who is fifth generation of Granny Truganini. Jim and Margaret have three fine children who are helping them do wonderful work. Jim's mother's mother is Granny Mary Clarke, third generation from Granny Truganini, whose true stories will never die out but will live on handed down. Let the happenings and the brutalities of the past be a lesson in how to build better relationships between all races.

Bill Onus was another great worker for Aboriginal affairs, so was his brother Eric and his wife. He went to school at Cummeragunja while I was there. Bill had an art shop in Belgrave where he sold artefacts. It was a rallying place for all of us Aborigines in the late 1940s and 1950s. Bill had one son and two daughters by his first wife (who was my first cousin): one has passed on, leaving a daughter Christina, who studied at a technical college in Melbourne. I believe Bill would have been a great asset today had he lived, in helping bring understanding on both sides, dark and white. Many Aborigines worked together at that time to bring understanding between dark and white Australians: Bill Onus, Harold Blair, Uncle Bill Cooper and Mr and Mrs Caleb Morgan. We began to realise that we Aborigines could voice our people's need for equal opportunities.

On quite a few weekends, Bill Onus would invite our Aboriginal women's musical group to entertain at his Aboriginal art shop, situated in the most wild and beautiful bushy surroundings. It was a never-ending source of wonder, even to the city Aborigines: the beautiful bark paintings, different makes of spears, nulla nullas, message sticks, totem poles and boomerangs of different makes from different tribes. Bill Onus had boomerang-throwing down to a fine art, and we never tired of watching him. He loved throwing them and showed that he loved it. We even had competitions throwing the boomerang at Cummeragunja and we became reasonably good. He would tell the white people (from all nationalities) who he invited out to this art shop of his work and interesting tales about each article and how our people used them. He had a little platform, like a stage, where corroborees, native songs and other entertainment was performed. That is where Jessie Taylor, Joyce Johnson and her daughter Winnie, Eric Onus, myself and others would sing numbers accompanied by the piano accordion, guitars and ukuleles. Bill and Eric Onus and some Lake Tyers Aborigines played the gum leaf. We performed Aborigine songs and dances. We loved expressing our stories of joys and sadness in this way.

One particular Sunday afternoon, Bill asked us to go out as usual. We loved it also because we met many visiting celebrities, including that great brave man Alan Marshall who wrote *I Can Jump Puddles*. I feel he has inspired a lot of people to forget our aches and pains. He was so nice and dignified. I don't even remember him being in a wheelchair. Other people we met were from overseas: white and dark New Zealanders with whom we made friends and asked out one evening to meet some of our people. It was at Alex and Meryl Jackamos's lovely home. They put on a lovely evening for everyone, like they always do. That was about eighteen years ago. We sang some native songs and got to know one another.

I remember asking one of the visitors (white) to speak and tell us about the work they were doing. They seemed good, genuine sorts.

To my surprise, one of the ladies stood up; everyone was quiet and listened to what she had to say. Her husband, who had been a wing commander in the Second World War, was there with her. These are some of the words she said, which I will never forget. It was the first time I had heard such words said to us. As every white and Aborigine listened, she thanked the host and hostess for being in their home, for meeting our people, and for the opportunity to say, from her heart, that she 'wished to apologise for white people's treatment of the Australian Aboriginal race, and would we please forgive?' She felt that we white and dark Australians could work together to make Australia the land that God meant it to be. Then we could be an example to the world in the way we lived. It touched my heart, and the hearts of many there that evening.

After that she made friends and visited our homes many times, having cups of tea, taking us for drives and having meals in her lovely home. That great friend and white sister, Jean Roberts, has passed on, leaving a son who is now doing worthwhile work as a university lecturer in Papua New Guinea. Eric Roberts, her husband, is known to Aborigines far and wide. Eric just had his eighty-third birthday.

I never cease to be thankful for meeting such people, black and white, from far and near. They not only spoke of change in their lives and in their homes but showed that it could be lived all over the world: not only by whites, but by all races, especially Aboriginals. It is a challenge, it is hard, but it has given me a clearer vision of what we are doing to our world (pornography, hate, greed and selfish ambition destroying each other). There is a right way to live and a wrong way, which is self-righteous and phoney.

When Harold Blair, the Aboriginal singer, first came to Melbourne from Queensland, Marjorie Lawrence, the famous Australian soprano gave him great praise and encouragement to be trained. We were very proud of him, and still are proud of him and his family. However, he tried to train an Aboriginal choir, here in Melbourne. He trained us wonderfully, even though we were not all gifted in reading music. He had a great sense of humour that kept us on tenterhooks. One night we were rehearsing when he stopped us in the middle of a tricky song. He pointed his baton at me and said, in a stern voice, 'Mrs Tucker'. As I was conscious of doing my best, I was keyed-up and hated to be scolded in front of the choir. I said, 'Yes', just as curtly. There was silence; everyone was listening. He grinned and said, 'You remind me of my mother'. I just gasped, and said to myself, 'I wish you were my son, too, I'd spank you for frightening me'. I thought I'd been doing something wrong! But it meant a lot to hear him say that, because his mother was a great person.

Harold Blair got to know us all and was eager to help us out in almost anything. He was the escort of one of my daughter's bridesmaids; she had four. His wife and children are a family to be proud of. His wife, Dorothy, also had a glorious singing voice. However, as human nature would have it, someone else wanted to form an Aboriginal choir, and the choir split in two (I must say, in fairness, not a white person either).

Harold Blair formed an organisation to help Aboriginal people who, let's face it, did not have food or material goods of any description. Being an extremely busy young man, he left most of the organising to myself, Mrs Una Hyland and another white man. We sorted clothes and whatnot to give to the needy Aborigines of that time. It was my first experience of white people's giving. I learned that white Australians can be generous, and many have been true friends to the Aboriginal race.

Time went on. I felt restless. I had tried everything, and we were still muddled, troubled, fighting and divided: Black against white and white against Black. I have long since discovered it is encouraged by people of both races who wish to divide and destroy for greedy ends. It is human nature. I am no different from anyone else—no better—might be worse! I get apprehensive in what I feel and think. What would have happened if God didn't give his only son Jesus to die on the cross? Let's face it, he paved the way of real love, truth, giving and living. Anyway, it is an answer to me. It wakes me up to the fact that when I am mean, unkind, misunderstanding and pigheaded it is because I don't want to give up my easy human nature. I do love my country and people—what am I doing to it by dwelling on past history and creating hate and bitterness? Let that kind of feeling 'go to Hell', where it belongs.

As it is said, the wheels of time turn and turn. Harold Blair went to America. His wife and some of our choir saw him off at Essendon airport. I wept as I saw that great plane going up into nowhere and was afraid for him. We were fond of him. His wife was standing there. She laughed at me kindly and said, 'Goodness, it should be me crying, not you'. I have tried to stop being an emotional sort of person, but I still am.

Meanwhile, we Aboriginal people were still drawn together. We would go to Pastor Doug Nicholl's church in Gore St, Fitzroy, and have times of singing old tunes and learning new ones. White people were invited as well, and a white woman played the organ. Pastor Doug Nicholls was a happy sort of man. Today, he and Lady Nicholls are doing great work. Doug has come a long way since he was a little fellow going to school with us at Cummeragunja.

When Harold arrived back from America, he seemed different, happier somehow. He rang me up one day and asked me whether I would like to go to America, and that I was invited as a delegate to the Moral Re-Armament training centre on Mackinac Island, Michigan. I just couldn't believe it, and I said, 'What on earth for?' and 'For how long?'

'About as long or as short as you wish to stay,' he replied.

I thought it was too good to be true. I thought every thought possible. I thought, 'What for?' I felt that I was an ignorant, uneducated, good-time person and an Aboriginal in her fifties. I felt I should settle down. But settle down to what? Besides, I suffered from claustrophobia, and couldn't fly shut up in an aeroplane way up in space.

I had to make my mind up, and only had ten days to do it. It meant leaving my family and my country. Such mixed feelings. What about seeing America and travelling? These ambitious thoughts won. With misgiving and wondering about what was to come, I decided to go.

Chapter Fifteen

The morning I left I didn't have time to think—trying to get a taxi to take me to the aerodrome. For a time, it looked like I might not make it. Everyone in the family was running around looking or phoning for a taxi, until someone saw a gentleman getting ready to go to work. We asked him to help me get to the aerodrome. I was very grateful to him. I still don't know who he was. At the aerodrome I was too overwhelmed to shed my usual tears. My family would not own up to crying, even in their hard times they are a jolly lot. Barbara, my youngest granddaughter, was just three weeks old. My brother-in-law Selwyn and sister Geraldine and family arrived at the airport too late to say goodbye; but it was heart-warming to know later that they were there.

Well, for days I had been wondering how I was going to sit in a closed-in aeroplane. Conscious of the airtight windows, I wouldn't look around. When the door was closed, I gazed hard through the window and wished that there was air coming through it. There were seven in the delegation: a couple from Newcastle, a young Aboriginal man from Perth, from Melbourne a businessman Mr Allchin, Mr Jim Ramsay, later a member of Parliament, and a young nurse, Lorna White. I must say, all my fears about air travel were at an end when Lorna turned on the air vent overhead. I marvelled at the comforts and care of the hostess when we changed at Sydney into a Qantas plane for my first flight over the ocean. Well, I just cannot describe it all; the sea, the clouds, what a long way down it was to fall; but I felt God had a mission for me and I was fairly comforted. My faith was not always strong, it was mostly in myself. I wondered at times why God really did bother?

Fiji was a place I had read about, but I did not think I would ever see it. I was very anxious to ask a lot of questions. The Fijians looked like a shy and proud people. However, our stay was short. We boarded the plane again and everyone was made comfortable. The next hop was a long one. A few had extra seats and could stretch out. I had three seats near the window. The hostess asked me if I would like to lie down and gave me cushions, but I sat up and looked out the window. It was all so exciting, and I wasn't sleepy. We were two hours out, when I saw one of the propellers stop turning and heard a loud crack, like lightning before a thunderstorm. I am sure I must have gone white with fright. My first words were, 'Please Lord, save us'. My instinct was to awaken Lorna and my other friends. Then I thought, 'Let them sleep, the captain and crew will surely know what to do'. Anyway, it was a matter of moments before the word came over the loudspeaker saying we were turning back to Fiji airport. I was glad to reach good old earth again.

We stayed the night in Fiji and next day boarded the mended plane with a little misgiving, but I felt the officers and crew knew what they were doing. Funny thing, the same thing happened on the other side of the plane; a propeller went bung. However, I heard it said that the plane could fly with two propellers if the others went bung. Well, we had to stay at Qantas's expense for about forty hours till the plane was OK to go again. There were tours and sightseeing. We had a delightful visit to a Fijian village and the children sang for us. We inspected the home of a chief and had an interesting time there.

I did not have any fears that any more propellers would break, but it was good to stretch our legs on Canton Island. The island is only seven miles wide and I thought the plane was going to land in the sea when it descended. I had never experienced such heat as when we were walking to the little building for a cuppa or a cool drink. I was glad to get back into the dear old plane, which I was getting very much attached to. When we reached Honolulu, where we left the plane, it was almost a feeling of regret, like leaving an old friend. When we reached the last step of the gangway, it was a delight to have the air hostess put a Hawaiian lei round my neck, beautiful fresh flowers, frangipani I think they were. It took all my time to keep watch where I was to go with my friends. My eyes were here, there and everywhere, taking everything in. There were a lot of interesting people at the airport. I was interested in the women with long dresses called *muumuus*. Some of them were very pretty, depending, I think, on whether you were slim or not.

We went to a hotel on Waikiki Beach near Diamond Head. The ocean looked better than any I'd ever seen, and the eats were something! Well, I was quite willing to sample; I've not seen watermelon so red before. I looked at Lorna's face, but she didn't look interested in such things. We had a lovely bedroom each and were much rested. Then on to another plane for [the] United States of America. Honolulu was so glamorous, the Hawaiians a mixed race and so interesting. Oh, what did I do to deserve this wonderful trip?

On to San Fransisco. We had a three-hour stopover and some friends took our party in their cars to visit their lovely city. Not far out of the airport we passed an avenue of beautiful gum trees that made me homesick. We were told that they were planted in memory of Australians who fought in the war. We drove across the Golden Gate Bridge and saw that renowned Alcatraz prison. We had a few pleasant moments and a cup of tea at one of these caring folks' homes, then back to the airport. Next stop, Chicago. I saw a few Negroes who looked as though they were not very interested in seeing another coloured sister from somewhere else; I guess they must see plenty.

Our last port of call: Mackinac Island. I cannot express my feelings; it was as though I was in another world. I had not experienced anything like this in my life. People, hundreds of them. Well! I have seen and mixed with a crowd of people before, but these were all different colours and nationalities, and many in their beautiful national costumes. I was told that there were at least sixty nationalities, many of them youth leaders, some leaders in their own country. This made me want to shrink up or sneak away. I did feel inferior. I didn't have a national costume of any distinction. My education was nil—only to the third grade. I didn't have riches or status. I was just an unknown Aborigine. I was introduced to this one and that. Oh, they were all gracious. I shrank back into my shell and didn't want to come out of it.

My first meal after arriving on this beautiful little island was in a unique building constructed like a monstrous Red-Indian tepee or wigwam. We were allotted to our meal tables in three huge dining rooms. It was a big job, as there were three or four thousand people. I began to wonder what I was over there for. My fear and inferiority mounted. And then I was led to a long, beautifully laid table. I cannot describe its beauty. I (an Aborigine) had eaten at high-class restaurants, hotels and receptions. I was proud of that fact. But this was something! There was a beauty about the atmosphere, the flowers! Any dumbbell or the maid-of-all-works could tell that the silver and cutlery was second to none. I learned that there were three huge dining rooms, all the same. This dining room was the biggest, and called Frank Buchman Dining Room, after the founder of Moral Re-Armament.

A feeling of pride came over me and I thought to myself, 'I'll show them an Australian Aboriginal has dignity and knows how to eat and conduct herself'. I was seated between two gentlemen who were really friendly, and I began to feel at ease, until one was introduced as Commander So-and-so! Then the other gentleman was introduced as Lord So-and-so. The gentleman on the other side of the table was jet black, beautifully dressed and so charming. He was Prince So-and-so from some part of Africa. I was introduced by my tribal name, Lilardia, that was given by a dearly loved old warrior Uncle Bill Cooper. My mother being in the line of Chiefs in her Ulupna tribe, I, being the oldest of her children, was given the honorific title Princess Lilardia. (In truth, every tribe has the right to hand down this title to the leaders of their tribe, if wished. Many different feelings I have had when I considered that honour—of my tribe and my mother.) Well, when I realised who these gentlemen were, and saw how naturally they behaved, I was struck dumb.

Later, some Maoris arrived, and I clung to their friendship. Their humour and ways were a little like Aboriginal people. I was lonely and felt inferior, not being as educated as they were. These Maoris spoke their own language to each other and wore their native costume. I realised that our Aboriginal culture and way of life was dying out fast, especially in Victoria and New South Wales. Lots of our children today do not know one word of their own particular tribal language. In the past, we thought that it was better to forget our traditions, culture and language. As a child, young as I was then and as old as I am now, I do not remember seeing my people dressed in anything but European (white people's) cast-off clothing. Unless they were working, then they would buy clothes, but rarely. Women were given government material and would be taught to cut out and sew by the manager's wife. They learned very quickly. They did not know what it meant to be ashamed of their bare nakedness but covered up where necessary with kangaroo and possum skins, which are especially warm in the winter. I believe the Supreme Being's teachings were with most of our tribes all through the ages.

However, the people at this conference were all just as much in need of answers for their country as I was. Great men and women leaders of great nations (which I didn't know existed!) in striking costumes: big, wonderfully dignified men, Arabs in flowing white robes and head gear, whom I learned were leaders of their countries, all wanting to find the answer to hate, bitterness and greed. But I was deeply troubled and ashamed to mix with them. I listened to stories of ordinary, unheard-of people giving all they had to right wrongs in their country.

I roomed with Lorna White, an Australian nursing sister, who had travelled with me. But being troubled by my old suspicions of white people, I kept with the group of happy Maoris. They gave a display of their culture, the *haka* and *poi* dances, which everyone enjoyed. I did feel that the people at the conference would have enjoyed our Australian stories of the old hunting days and today's Aboriginal life. I felt a bit of jealousy on behalf of my country then. My goodness, I had a lot to learn, and I felt it.

I attended lectures and meetings telling of tragic true happenings from the French people during the war. I heard Madame Irene Laure, who was a resistance fighter in France. She hated the Germans with all her heart. The Germans had tortured her son, in her presence, to make them tell secrets of the resistance movement. She told of how she could not stand to be in the same room as a German without wanting to vomit. Once, in Germany, when a group of German diplomats were on the platform, she had walked out of the assembly. But before she got to the door, Dr Buchman spoke to her and asked her how she could build a new world without the Germans? How could this be done if one nation was left out?

She rushed to her room and started to pack her belongings to leave, tears running down her face. She stayed in her room two or three days, thinking. Then she heard that the Germans were speaking. This French woman, who wasn't a resistance fighter for nothing, came to the hall, went to the platform and shook hands with each of those Germans. Tears running down her cheeks, she apologised to them for the hate and bitterness in her heart. I heard that the late Chancellor Adenauer invited her to Germany. She told us that she cried when she saw the German women looking for lost possessions in their bombed homes, pitifully picking up this and that in the rubble. She went among them and talked. Chancellor Adenauer said that she was one of the best ambassadors France had ever had. Madame Laure came to Australia once that I know of. I hope she comes again and stays longer.

Another happening that I saw and heard with my own ears was a Japanese officer telling his story to a vast audience, including some Americans in uniform. I could scarcely breathe, fearing for this Japanese officer on the platform as he told how, during the war, a young American airman was brought to him. The young American's plane had been shot down, and he was badly hurt. This officer said that he did not give him care; he just made him a prisoner of war. This Japanese officer really did look miserable when he said that he did not know if the American died. He had also been mixed up in shady deals after the war, as he had access to Red Cross funds. What it must have cost him to lay his soul bare! I can still see how this young fellow finished, by asking that huge audience to forgive him, saying that he wanted to give his life to undo what he had done by fighting for world peace, or something like that. When he sat down, you could hear a pin drop. I know I was so deeply touched that I cried and shook like a jelly. I felt he was so courageous. Then the whole audience stood up and clapped and clapped. It upset my whole world; I thought a lot would be mad with him! Then out of the standing crowd, an American airman strode up to the platform. He apologised for his and his comrade's actions during the occupation of Japan; how they did wrong things, violating Japanese girls and giving them babies and whatnot.

Mackinac was truly a heavenly, peaceful place. It was autumn and the golden and red autumn leaves against the blue of the lake made an absolute picture. There were no cars allowed on this island, only horse-drawn carriages and, in winter, sleighs drawn by horses in the snow.

After three weeks of being on that lovely island, I got homesick and was determined to go home. I was restless and felt subconsciously that I was a fraud in my make-up. I could not run away from that feeling. Everyone was wonderful as they got to know me. Some were pretty straight with me, especially a young man called Peter Barnet, who would always point out how over-packed my poor little handbag was (I still indulge in over-packing). The meals were out of this world and I was enjoying them to the full. I remember having meals with two Australians and one Canadian doctor and their wives. One of the doctors passed me the dish of ice cream and fruit. I said, 'Oh, this is lovely, I'll have to go on a diet!' I was plump as it was. Straight away a doctor said, 'Would you like to?' Untruthfully, I said, 'Yes', so, pointing to the Diet Kitchen, he said, 'I'll fix up a diet chart for you'. That was one of the Australian doctors, Dr Christopher Lancaster. When I returned

Margaret planting a eucalypt at 'Armagh', Melbourne,
in honour of Queen Salote of Tonga.

to Australia, I visited their home many times, and when their children were small, they would ask our Aboriginal children out to stay for the weekend, bless them.

As I was saying, I felt homesick and if I could have gone and walked home across the lake and the ocean I would have! Wishful thinking. However, my friend Lorna who travelled over with me from Australia said, 'Come down under the tree overlooking the lake, sit on the comfortable seats and think quietly, asking for God's guidance'.

'All right,' I said, 'But what I want to do is to go back home to my people and my family, who need me I'm sure'. I didn't say that I was getting letters from back home saying that they were all right. When my daughter, Mollie, was working late, Aunty Sarah Cooper, Uncle Bill's widow, was caring for the household. Aunty Sarah would have been in her late sixties then. The baby was cared for by Mrs Murphy, a very dear neighbour. Alan, my son-in-law, was in a good job.

So, I sat under that shady tree overlooking the Great Lakes with Lorna. I repeatedly said, 'I want to go home'. I did not know why I felt so uncomfortable. It wasn't loneliness, there were plenty of younger and older Australians. As I sat there thinking, I heard Lorna's quiet voice coming through my thinking, 'Let's get some guidance from God, he will tell us what to do'. I thought, 'Goodness me, of course he'll tell me to go home. I'm sure he only wants good, highly educated people of note here'. So, for the first time, God really did come into my heart. For the first time I realised what Moral Re-Armament meant. I do remember a feeling came to me, that I had to stay. I felt how selfish I was, and had been, not giving to humanity, and least of all to my family, the things that really mattered most in the world. Not mushy love and affection that drew them all to me, but what God wanted me to do. Then, in a flash, I saw a picture of myself; I wasn't perfect. I was proud, and proud of my race and what I was doing for them. Then I heard Lorna's voice, saying, 'What did God say to you?'

I said, 'Stay long enough, for fun'. I stayed just on eight months, and when I think back it truly was fun.

I didn't dwell on the things that I was ashamed of. I made use of it in a way that helped other people. For the first time I allowed my hair to go back to its real colour, though I felt awful with shame when some girls in the ladies' 'tidy' room said to me, 'Oh, your hair has some red parts'. I always kept my hair real black with colour out of the bottle whenever I saw streaks of grey showing. So, I answered offhandedly, 'Oh yes, a lot of my people have red hair, light hair and such'. Afterwards I did ask God to forgive me for such a silly lie, and openly said what I had done with my hair. I was amazed how I liked the grey that was naturally coming. Of course, a lot of my people, having white fathers or mothers, were adorned with red, brown and black hair, but they also had the skin colour to go with it.

I began to realise that Moral Re-Armament was an old truth. I felt it was Christianity practised in real life, starting with oneself. Everything I had believed about Christianity was now upside down, which was indeed a challenge. I still got fidgety when I could not understand or grasp some things. I was glad to meet Australians, especially delighted to meet Mr Kim Beasley Snr. I met him on the day he was leaving to go back home to Australia. Then I felt even more homesickness, but I was learning that how I lived and what I gave was important. America gave me so much: I felt that it would be a joy to repay in the same way.

I was invited to take part in an African play called *The Last Phase*, which depicted the story of a country in Africa and the moral qualities needed to make that country work. I thought that I still looked like an Aboriginal, even in the African costume and headgear. I had two words to say, which was thrilling because I got to learn what it was all about. Other coloured people were also asked to help. I can remember a pretty Indian girl of about fourteen, her mother was a member of parliament in New Delhi. She came to me one day with a solemn face, and in her quaint English she said, 'Mrs Tucker, I wish to apologise to you'.

I said, 'What on earth for?'

She told me that when she first saw me in African costume she had laughed. She thought that I looked funny. I told her that I laughed when I saw myself in the mirror as well. I felt that I didn't look much like an African. The Africans helped me with the play, and I soon caught on.

I took part in another play while I was in America, in Atlanta, Georgia. It was called *The Crowning Experience* and it was the true story of the life of a Negro woman, Mary McLeod Bethune. She was the only child, in her family of sixteen, born out of slavery. She was the youngest, and fortunate in having been educated. She started a school herself, built from bits and pieces from the rubbish dump. They made pencils from pieces of charred wood.

The Crowning Experience has now been made into a film. I have seen it fifteen or twenty times on screens across Australia, New Zealand, Fiji and Tonga. I love it! Real human plays and films like this shock you into reality, and out of that comfortable feeling that you are a good person with nothing to worry about. Moral Re-Armament showed me that Black, white, yellow, no matter what colour, our human nature was the same! How small our thinking is when we let colour, nationalities or position divide us.

Mary McLeod Bethune's education had built her character. It made her a whole person, using her heart as well as her brain. She was prepared to make sacrifices and to right wrongs, especially things that she had done herself. I have done many wrong and really silly things. I was beginning to feel that there was something in this Moral Re-Armament way of life. I had many Moral Re-Armament friends who patiently explained things and stuck with me. Oh, I had my moments and days of tantrums. I wanted to escape by going home to Australia. But then I realised that I couldn't escape from my human nature. It came to me that even I, an unknown Aborigine, could give this precious gift to her people who were hungry for knowledge.

I left America after eight months. The flight to Manila was great, everyone in the plane was like one big happy family. We touched down at Guam and got out to stretch our legs. I can remember Jean Hughes and I walked around this little island and I gathered some shells. I put them in my hanky and tied it up. I thought they were so pretty.

We got back to the plane. When I put my hanky with the shells into my handbag, I gave a little shriek. The hanky was moving about! Yes, one shell was occupied!

We arrived at Manila and were all taken to our respective hotels. One could see dreadful war damage—sunken ships and bombed areas all around. I heard tales of dreadful happenings, cruelty, torture, hate and bitterness. On a clear day, one could see Corregidor, where the Americans and others had lost their lives fighting for all they held dear.

It was Easter and I do remember making many Filipino friends. One family with whom I made friends was Captain Agerico Palaypay, who had been aide-de-camp to President Magsaysay, until the president was killed in an air crash. I was thrilled and humbled when Captain Palaypay's wife asked me to stay with them next time I was over in the Philippines. I felt like a queen, the way I was treated. I was humbled some more when, as an Australian, I was asked to lay a wreath on the tomb of President Magsaysay.

Rajmohan Gandhi, a grandson of Mahatma Gandhi, was chairman of a televised discussion between all the different nationalities from the conference. I was representing my country, Australia, but when I found out that I had to speak on air, I was terrified. I couldn't think what to say and my mind went blank. I felt I would be letting people down everywhere. Then, my word, I prayed and asked God to tell me what to say. Then I looked around the room and noticed everyone in the room was doing the same thing. So, I forgot myself and prayed for them. A miracle happened; I lost any fear and gave with real joy in my heart.

We also visited and stayed at Baguio in the mountains. While in the Philippines, at conferences, I witnessed many Filipinos and Japanese apologising to each other. Filipinos telling of their former hatred for the Japanese; doctors and Heads of State with tears running down their cheeks, both Japanese and Filipino. I cried with joy to see that God can obliterate hate, no matter what the nationality.

After ten days, Jean Hughes and I boarded the plane for Darwin. When I saw the shores of my homeland through the plane window, my heart melted. I cried and thanked God for giving me another chance to bring understanding between all people. We landed in Darwin, had time for lunch and a shower, then caught a plane for Sydney. I stopped with a friend and her dear mother, who has passed on now. I was overwhelmed by the number of dark and white friends I met during that brief stay before flying to Melbourne. The folks back home, how dear they were to me. I never thought I could live without being near them; yet I had been away eight months. It dawned on me how dearly God Almighty cared for everyone. I couldn't get home quickly enough. At Essendon, I saw Black people, and white people painted Black, doing a corroboree to welcome me home. In the confusion I did not recognise which were my grandchildren. My daughter and the rest of my clan were all there and it was a joy to see them.

There was a welcome home event for us at 'Armagh', the Moral Re-Armament headquarters in Toorak. It was the most beautiful home I had ever seen in Australia, with a dignified reception room and magnificent chandeliers. I didn't know that my friend and I were the guests of honour, but I can remember speaking with assurance and without fear for the first time. I have stayed in this beautiful home many times, as did my mother. She said that Moral Re-Armament was like a big stone, going around the world killing all evil.

The host and hostess that welcomed us to that regal home were Colonel the Hon. Malise Hore-Ruthven and Angela Hore-Ruthven and family. Colonel Hore-Ruthven was a brother of Lord Gowrie, former Governor General of Australia.

My daughter Mollie invited the Hore-Ruthvens to a meal in her three-bedroom commission home in Broadmeadows (that was about sixteen years ago). I didn't think she would manage: 'Oh ye of little faith', that was me! I said, 'Oh no, Mollie', thinking of the lovely silver dishes, cutlery, dinner sets and whatnot at 'Armagh' (all the gifts of people who were grateful to Moral Re-Armament). 'Well,' Mollie said, 'They are always asking us to a meal, and the kiddies for weekends, and they make us feel like royalty. We'll manage'. And manage she did, with a borrowed dinner set and cutlery sets from the neighbours (white) who were just as thrilled as we were when they accepted the invitation. The colonel and his wife, son James and two daughters Nancy and Sally, Mr Eric Turpins, an Irishman and another person, I cannot remember his name. They all came. I will never forget that crowded dining room, with Mollie, Alan, old Aunty Sarah Cooper, myself and all the kids (all steps and stairs kids because there were a few adopted ones). These white friends were great fun and on many occasions were out to visit little Osway Street, Broadmeadows. They took our unruly children for the weekend and drives, and believe me, our kiddies were not angels, far from it!

In 1975, I received a letter from Nancy Hore-Ruthven that brought back memories of that visit. It said, 'I have one wonderful memory of your mother, Marg. We went to Mollie's home, as you describe, for a meal. Your mother was there. She was sitting in a straight-backed chair surrounded by children, dogs, noise and general family bric-a-brac. When we came in, we went up to her and she said, 'Welcome to my home and my land'. She said it with such power and simplicity … she was a queen sitting there on her chair, and no-one in Australia had even said, 'Welcome to my country', to us before. It made a deep impression on me.

I can remember one young friend, a young man, would arrive in his car to take the boys for a drive. Maxine, my oldest granddaughter, aged nine then, would say, 'Please come in. I'll make you a cup of tea'. He would come in and have a cuppa that Maxine insisted on making herself.

Many Australians and people from all over the world, as I have already told, were looking for answers to problems in families and the world's problems. One family, Tom and Florence Uren, took an Aboriginal family into their home, a family with five children and another on the way. The father, like a lot of dads, liked his firewater and once or twice came home worse for wear. He was given a straight talk and was told how he was letting the family down. But most of all, he was cared for and looked after. He gave the drink away and his mates scoffed at him and said, 'Oh, you are weak'. He just grinned at them as

Margaret with her MBE.

he drank his lemonade and said, 'Lions and tigers are strong, and they drink water'. When his wife was taken to hospital to have their sixth child (now thirteen), Tom and Florence were there too. This Aboriginal family was helped to get work and a home. The Aboriginal mother is a great worker, not only for her people, but for white people too. She does great work visiting gaols, seeing Aboriginal prisoners.

People like Tom and Florence, Jim Beggs of the Waterside Workers Federation and his family, and many more like these ordinary people have shown me in how they lived that, 'God so loved the world that he gave his only begotten son that who soever believeth in him should not perish but have everlasting life'. I have learned to hit out straight at wrong things, and put right what I have done wrong, no matter what. Believe me, it has been hard. I've cried buckets of tears and suffered hell; but thank God I can always start again. I have wonderful friends, black and white, that understand and encourage me to keep going. I can never reach such heights as perfection, but great results happen in trying. I might say, as an Aboriginal person, I have my moments of very bitter frustration. I am thankful for the simple truth of knowing what is right and wrong. Everyone has the right to make that decision, rich or poor. There is only one source of richness, the richness of caring and giving love.

After returning home from America in 1958, I was elected by the governor and council to serve on the Aborigines Welfare Board, which was situated in Lonsdale Street at that time. My goodness, I felt so humbled that I was chosen. I was the first Aboriginal woman to be appointed. Pastor Nicholls and Harold Blair had been on it and were a great asset, but me; I was dumb for the first couple of months. The chairman was very understanding and helpful. I must say I was 'hauled over the coals' more than once to explain some distorted tales, which I find happens to downgrade people. I was very happy on the Aborigines Welfare Board, which I felt was genuine and was very sorry to see it break up. I learned a great deal and we at the Aboriginal United Council of Women [United Council of Aboriginal and Islander Women] gave Mr Harry Davey a big farewell reception.

Chapter Fifteen

Our new Ministry for Aboriginal Affairs, of which Mr Reg Worthy was the director, was totally different. The old Welfare Board really gave what I felt was love and care to each Aboriginal family and disciplined them individually. Under the old, kindly methods of the Welfare Board, we paved the way for better conditions for Aboriginal people, the start of better schooling and housing. But years bring changes and our needs as Aboriginals changed too. Most struck out for higher education, equal opportunities and rights.

Mr Worthy had a gigantic job to do, putting new policy forward. He did his best. I must admit that I had to learn all over again and must have made myself obnoxious asking too many questions. I realise the tremendous opportunities that are before people like me, and I am the least brainiest. But when I do care for people from my heart, a new world opens up to me. Such a great deal has been given to me, and I do want to share it with everyone. One of the gifts given to me and my people was the MBE. Without the loving upbringing of my mother, those wonderful missionaries, and the loving togetherness of my Aboriginal people, I wouldn't have got through many hardships.

Before I became a member of the Welfare Board I had a lovely trip to New Zealand. We visited Auckland, Wellington, Dunedin, Christchurch: beautiful, God-given places. I met many Maoris, including Major Harawira and his wife. He had been chaplain to a Maori battalion. Mrs Wiki Bennett MBE was another one I met, and Guide Rangi. My friends and I visited and stayed in their homes and spoke in schools.

Another wonderful experience was going to Tonga with Miss Silvia Cust, an Australian, and a group of New Zealanders, both white and dark. The late great Queen Salote, who had seen the film *The Crowning Experience* while she was on holiday in Auckland, invited us to show it to her people. The queen and her son Prince Tungi (as he was then) housed us in a guesthouse and had her own home helpers look after us. We were invited to her palace to have morning tea and have our photos taken with her. We made friends with her turtle, the one Captain Cook had given to her grandfather or great-grandfather. It died a few weeks after the queen died. I did enjoy that Easter in Tonga. That huge church, the singing, the trumpets and other music, the queen herself taking part, I will never forget.

The Crowning Experience had several sessions. The hall was big, but not huge enough for to fit the schools and colleges in one session. All the people wanted to billet us in their homes. They gave us wonderful hospitality and showered gifts on us, even though we begged them not to, and said we would need a ship to carry them back to Australia!

One morning the queen visited us at her guesthouse where we were staying. She was most gracious and had a cup of tea with us. We showed her another film, *The Men of Brazil*, while she was with us. I remember her majesty saying, 'We haven't much money, but we have God'. We said farewell, and a great crowd came to see us off at the airport, miles out of the city. Even the matron of the hospital came to farewell us. Our dear friends, the Tongan women, farewelled us with a dance. The three-hour flight to Suva was rough going, with rain and storms. I admit it frightened the devil out of me and I prayed to God that we would reach Suva. It stormed so much that the pilot had words that we may have to avert the flight to Nadi. But prayers were answered, and we were able to land. It was a small plane that carried just a dozen people and the crew. We showed *The Crowning Experience* that night and had supper at the Fijian mayor's home. Later we visited schools and both Fijian and Indian homes.

On my first visit to Brisbane for an MRA conference, my friend Jean and I stayed with Barbara Groves, her husband and family. Wonderful people, people that you meet once, and even if you do not see them again for ten or twenty years you know they will welcome you and open not only their doors, but their hearts. Mrs Groves's parents had a seaside home at Buderim, which they offered to Colonel and Mrs Hore-Ruthven for a little holiday, and they said they would be so happy to have me along for a holiday with them. I loved this family by this time, they were such a wonderfully sincere, lovable, happy family.

Margaret in New Zealand, patting a kiwi.

They shared their joys, their up and doings with everyone they came in contact with. They made you feel that you were 'leading the way' in every good thing that happened.

I'll not forget begging them to let me do the washing, feeling so happy that at least I could do something I was sure of. I wasn't at the wash tub very long before Mrs Hore-Ruthven (she came from a high-up family too) was begging me to let her help me with the washing. Grudgingly I said, 'Bless you, would you like to hang them out?' I carried the basket and she happily hung them out. I was a little bit outraged when Mr Turpin came into the laundry and showed me how to scrub the collars with a soft brush that he had for the purpose, so as not to wear them out. However, I went to get the clothes in, and I giggled at the way the shirts and other articles were hung. I can't begin to tell! But my heart melted and I thought to myself, 'You lovely, precious person, wanting to help me with the washing', and here were the clothes pegged in such a comical way. I thought, 'Everyone to their station'. The story brought much merriment to the dinner table when I apologised for being such a know-it-all. Mrs Hore-Ruthven laughed the most.

On another day, we had lunch and spent a nice afternoon with Sir Raphael and Lady Cilento and grandchildren. Then we all went to the beach, not far from the house, and took off our shoes and stockings and paddled in the water. Then we went back to the house. I played my ukulele and sang to her little grandchildren till my throat was dry. When I left, those little grandchildren hugged me and kissed me. I felt a little embarrassed, thinking their mother would mind, but she thanked me too.

Sir Raphael and Lady Cilento came to dinner and I found out that Sir Raphael knew Albert Namatjira, who was in trouble at the time for giving drink to his people. Even now I shed a tear and my heart aches when I think of it. Our people always share everything. I wrote a letter and gave it to Sir Raphael to give to Namatjira. I was glad to have word that it was delivered. I have met Namatjira and always feel grateful for meeting this tremendous personality, a good man. Thank God for what he gave humanity, black and white. I cannot help a feeling of pride that he was of my race.

One day, Colonel Hore-Ruthven and the family drove about fifty miles to visit a beautiful old homestead, over a-hundred-and-thirty-years old, their friends the Bell sisters owned it. Royalty such as the Prince of Wales, the Queen Mother and Lord Gowrie had stayed there. I didn't know all this when they asked me to go with them for a drive. I loved nothing better than a drive. Eric Turpin drove, taking turns with Nancy and James. It was a lovely drive, and when we neared this beautiful old homestead, they told me about their friends, whom they knew very well. Oh my, my thoughts were in turmoil. I was very worried for them, taking me along on this visit. I thought to myself, 'Oh, my goodness, what are they going to think of these great people having me, an Aboriginal, for a friend'. I had only been in this sort of home as a maid. I couldn't have my friends snubbed because of me, so I told them my feelings. Both cars stopped and we talked about it. I thought that if my friends wanted me on this visit, then I'll go with them. I prayed for courage.

When we arrived one of the ladies was waiting to greet Colonel Hore-Ruthven and his family. As she led the way, I hung back cowardly; or my pride reared its neck like a snake. This lady, the youngest of the Bell sisters, stopped and waited for me and talked with me as we walked into this beautiful old homestead. It was hot, and the luncheon was laid out on a table under a beautiful tall, bushy tree. The eats were delicious-looking, especially the lovely red sliced watermelon. The youngest of these Bell sisters got a slice of bread and she threw it into the air. In no time, birds were snapping up the bits of bread before they touched the ground. However, I thought to myself, 'Which part of the house is the kitchen? I'll probably be eating in there'. Then the older Bell sister, sitting at the top of the table, pointed everyone to their seat. She looked at me and said, 'You, Lilardia, will sit here', pointing to her right side. I got such a shock as I realised that I was the guest of honour! I felt so ashamed of myself, I could have cried. I didn't deserve it, having such sincere friends. Then, after lunch the youngest Bell sister took me into this lovely garden and showed me the different lovely trees that royalty had planted. The Prince of Wales, King George's son, his tree was tall. So was Lord Gowrie's, Colonel Hore-Ruthven's brother.

This great-hearted Bell sister then took me for a little walk away from the house and showed me two graves neatly fenced, some pretty greens growing inside. She told me that they were two Aboriginal women whom her mother loved. They were always with her. I lost all my pride then, and I got my ukulele out of the car and sat on the garden seat with all of them and sang Aboriginal songs and other songs. It was a great heart-melting time with these old pioneers, the Bell sisters. I told Colonel Hore-Ruthven that I thought I'd have to eat my meal in the kitchen on my own, and straight away Mrs Hore-Ruthven said that she would have had her meal in there too! I know that she meant it.

When the Hore-Ruthvens were asked to speak at the Sunday forum at Wesley Church, Melbourne, they had me speak as well. The Rev. Dr Sir Irving Benson was in charge of the church then. I had a heartfelt letter from him when my mother died.

Margaret at her mother's grave.

Chapter Sixteen

As I write it is 12 July 1974, our National Aborigines Day. What are we Aboriginal people making of this day? A few say it is a day of mourning. Some make it a day to voice political action, which is the trend of the last few years; or should I say the trend of many, many years. This had to come, and when you think of it, it has been there all the time, right through the years. Human nature! I remember the words I heard on Mackinac Island: 'If everyone cared enough and everyone shared enough—there would be enough for everyone's need, but not enough for everyone's greed'. And the home truth that has helped me the most: 'It is not the colour of one's skin that matters, it is character'.

I have always said, especially when trying to get a point across to a white person, 'Oh, you have to think like an Aborigine if you want to help our people'. Then it hit me, Heaven forbid, our Aboriginal people are humans, we are not a separate specimen. We have the same human nature, the same as any other race. We can all, with courage and thoughtfulness, put right what is wrong in our countries today, starting with ourselves.

I have to start with myself all the time. I am always saying in despair, 'Oh God, I want to tear so-and-so to pieces. He is hunting my people and there are only a few of us left. Our land has been taken, our hunting grounds, even our right to think for ourselves. Some of us are too afraid to open our mouths, and when we do, we are labelled radicals'. I feel despair and misery so deep I cannot even shed a tear. I do pray from my heart when I think of Jesus Christ and what he gave thousands of years ago to save people from being destroyed by evil in all its forms. Our wise old Aboriginal people used to say long ago, 'He did not leave one nation out of what he died for'. This is a truth that really counts.

As an Aboriginal thinking of my people that have gone, of the pioneers and convicts, my heart aches for the struggles and hardships caused by greed and cruelty in this country. I feel, on National Aborigines Day, that we must put aside our grievances and pay tribute to the old people by putting right what is wrong in our country today. Australia can be a pattern for the whole world in the way we live and give, especially in bridging the gap between black and white. We can do it together! We need to 'think bigger' from our hearts. Young Aboriginal people teach me a lot; they have great courage and give to our country in many ways.

Many changes have come in the years I have lived. I have memories of the cruelty, misery and frustrations but have found an answer to the hurts of the past. Wonderful happenings, such as finding relics all over Australia that prove that 40,000 years ago our people were not the least advanced after all. I for one, and many of our dark Australians, were very happy with the discovery and am grateful to know, from the findings of tribal graves, what happened in this God-given land thousands of years ago.

My old uncle who reared me told us where our tribal burial grounds were. When I was young, a white man, married to an Aboriginal woman, earned his living by digging up relics for the museum. He had come upon the vicinity of this tribal ground and was disciplined by old Uncle and given a terrible fright. He was told 'if he so much as put his feet on that sacred ground again, he would be finished good and proper'. He didn't. He said that he was more than sorry. So many mistakes in the past, so many mistakes in the present.

I find now that Aborigines all over Australia are one big tribe now. Tribes that lived on Moonahcullah married into tribes coming from Moulamein, Lake Boga, Swan Hill, Robinvale, Echuca, Barmah, Mooroopna and Shepparton. There were no state boundaries [in] those days, so our people travelled far and wide. Remnants of wonderful tribes at Warrnambool, Lake Condah and Heywood near Portland told stories of old beliefs and traditions, stories our people remember and believe. Although our people are marrying people of Aboriginal descent from all over Australia, many, many secrets of their folklore are being buried with the old people, or are seen as old-fashioned by our own youth; some of whom are being educated at university. It is a pity. This ancient knowledge is priceless and should be valued.

Sometimes when I am on my own, such thoughts come crowding into my head and heart. A great white man once told me that Aboriginal people could bring love, care and understanding to all people; bringing white people back to their faith. He also used to say that God gave us two ears and one month; so, listen more than you talk. I am conscious of talking too much sometimes. It is great to be quiet and listen, not only with your ears, but with your heart. The answers to great difficulties are given, if only we have the courage of our convictions. I am a bit of a coward and I do like my own way a lot of the time. But I have learned to make amends when I am wrong and say sorry from my heart. When I feel cross, I'd often like to do a 'wild corroboree', but as I understand and care for people more and more, the desire to do the wild corroboree diminishes. Hurts and fears from the past can be useful. We can learn from those mistakes; we may not forget but we can forgive.

I ponder over memories passed down from my mother, before Sturt and his explorers rowed down the Murray River. My old mother passed on stories of how our people watched them peacefully and some followed them unseen for miles on the banks of the river. I like to think the headmen of my mother's tribe influenced other tribes to let them go on their way peacefully. I do feel our old Aboriginal owners of this land were so much wiser than we Aboriginal descendants of today. I love my

Aboriginal people of today but wonder if, in another two hundred years, we will have been swallowed up by mixed marriages. Evil is the same today as it was a thousand years ago. The truth is the same and a lie is the same. I wonder, what we parents are giving the children of today? Mostly, 'Don't do what I do, do what I say'. There is a cure for this, simply having courage to fight for higher moral values. I find this hard sometimes, especially when my human nature goes haywire and I try to follow my own thinking, not measuring decisions on the basis of what is right.

Aboriginal people are mostly peace-loving, but always on their guard. Mostly we like to meet others halfway, I suppose all people do!

All my life it has been a joy to do things, from getting a sum right in school to taking a pretty nankeen (crane) feather to a young schoolteacher. But if I had to own up to a wrongdoing, no matter how small, I would ponder over it for days. Then it would get too much for my conscience and I would have to be honest. For most of my life I have tried to pitch in and help with this and that. It has been a fun, natural way of life. I try to fathom why one want to be the top dog. I suppose it is fear of losing prestige. Why is jealousy, envy, bitterness and hatred created? I have gone through all these miserable feelings and realise one can be so selfish and cowardly. My biggest fear in life is doing the wrong thing, because I am not happy until I put things right.

It is amazing what is happening now, compared with forty years ago. The Aboriginal health centre and Aboriginal legal aid are doing their best. I cannot help thinking that prevention is better than cure. The answer to all the misery in the world is absolute honesty, unselfishness, purity, love and care for all people from the heart. A man died on the cross long ago, giving up everything to show the way. I know people today who are trying to do the same. Call it what you like, but deep in my heart I do believe in the Holy Spirit, the Good Spirit, the wonderful spirit that has neither hate, bitterness, class or creed. Everyone has it in their heart, deep down, if we only skim all the scum off and get rid of feelings of bitterness, hate and the feelings of hopelessness, like I have been having in the last few years.

I try to keep out of mischief and to do what is right for the rest of my life. In this I am guided by the story Pastor Sir Douglas Nicholls told in church one day about a black American preacher who said, 'You can play a tune of sorts on the white keys of a piano; you can play some sort of tune on the black keys; but for perfect harmony, you must use both'. I got that point; it is a terrific one.

My first visit to beautiful Canberra was in the 1930s. We were presented to a Mr Johnson MP by our leader, Mr Shadrach James, son of our one-time schoolteacher Mr Thomas James of Cummeragunja. We travelled in a huge bus hired for the occasion. It was filled with Aboriginal women and a few men, mostly choir members. While on that visit, we were invited to sing on the radio for the first time (no TV then). We also got lost, our tracking instinct was hopelessly muddled in that lovely city. We slept in a dormitory at a boys' college, it being school holidays. We had a very interesting time with the Members of Parliament, whom I don't think took us very seriously. I also remember one calling me Princess, which reminded me to act like one. After all, didn't we come from the real owners of this country? Our leader, Shadrach James, spoke wonderfully. I remember being promised jobs to do way outback, visiting our Aboriginal people and seeing their needs. It didn't come to anything as far as I can remember, but we travelled to our homes with great expectations. We felt that something was attempted and tried.

We didn't see much of Canberra then, but some years later in the 1960s I attended a Moral Re-Armament conference. It was a great eye-opener for me. I loved every minute. It was very educational, especially meeting a great number of nationalities, Maoris, white New Zealanders, Indians, people from the Philippines. It was like one big happy family, everyone looked after and cared for each other. There were breaks for sightseeing, picnics and visiting embassies. That is when I met up with Blacks' Mountain. I am sorry that so-called progress and modern building, in the trend of the day, might destroy the look of this natural monument, our memories and real history that reaches tens of thousands of years. It was pointed out to me as we travelled around Canberra district, sightseeing. Hearing the name Blacks' Mountain, which I am told is now called Black Mountain, brought me back to when I was a child. My mother, around a campfire or in our little humpy, would always tell us stories (when we begged her to) about the olden times 'way back'. She told us what happened when she ran away from home and married a Murrumbidgee River Aborigine—my father, Billy Clements.

One of the true stories she told took place after she was married. Father felt he must take her to meet his tribe, his people around Yass and Gundagai: all Murrumbidgee district. I believe my old grandmother was a tall six-footer and a full-blooded black woman. Well, she was so happy and proud of her oldest son's new wife. She began to plan a walkabout here, there and everywhere to show her new daughter-in-law to other relations. One of these walks was to Blacks' Mountain, before Canberra was even thought of. Our people had their favourite camping ground at the foot of Blacks' Mountain. Game was plentiful, it was a happy place; one of the favourite spots of the Wiradjuri tribe. When my mother was taken there, I was three months on the way to being born; so, when Blacks' Mountain was shown to us my whole being was overjoyed. I do hope and pray that the name Blacks' Mountain will remain in my people's memories because it truly was an Aboriginal camping ground. Now I believe it is a caravan park for all people. I do not begrudge that, it is how it should be, a delightful, happy place for all people of all colours and nationalities: the world's family.

This inheritance, passed on to us, brings it home to us Aboriginal descendants; what riches in this God-given country that is ours. I have struggled all my life working, my mother before me and, yes, my grandmother; who could hardly speak English and worked for a bit of tucker. I feel so much that there is not one Aboriginal person who has not been through some sort of major tragedy in their lives. I do not write this down in bitterness, but with a plea for understanding. Give back to our people and families some of the inheritance that their great grandparents owned; not little bits of hand-outs. Let we Aboriginal remnants share equally this God-given land of ours. I say what my old mother used to say: 'don't feel sorry for yourselves, be up and doing'. Let us get together, black and white, people from all over the world care and share for humanity in the way God means us to care and share.

Note from a great-granddaughter

This new publication originated from generational wisdom that came first from Yamak, Theresa Clements ('Queen' or leader of the Ulupna clan), who was responsible for handing down knowledge to her first-born daughter, Margaret Tucker. This role was then passed down to Margaret Tucker's daughter, Mollie Dyer, and in turn to Mollie's first-born daughter Maxine Barr (my mum), and then to me, Tania Rossi (nee Burns). This continuous family line ensures that cultural stories and personal experiences are remembered. Some of these stories and their legacies are traumatic. Every generation of family members lives with the consequences of past events. Despite the trauma, all of these women endured and fought for their people.

Yamak was a medicine woman and midwife, working for her people and also with the white community. She was born on her Country and removed to Maloga Mission, then to Cummeragunja Aboriginal Station. She was again removed to Warangesda Mission, where she met her future husband William Clements, a Wiradjuri man. This book traces Nan Tucker's own experience of forced removal and her contribution to her community. Nan Tucker had a wide vision and had concern for all people regardless of their race, but at the forefront was finding a voice for her own people. Nanna Mollie grew up with her white grandparents.

Margaret Tucker with great-granddaughter Tania.

Being raised in white society had an enormous impact on her identity and relationships with her Aboriginal family. She didn't renew these important links until her middle age, when her work with Aboriginal children in the justice system revealed the need for Aboriginal childcare services. She would go on to form the Aboriginal Childcare Agency (now VACCA). Her idea was to keep children connected to their family and to maintain their lineage, which is essential to strong cultural identities.

Nana Mollie, like her mother, married a white man. They thought that their children would be safer from government removal and other harm if they didn't marry within their Aboriginal community, but this was not always the case. Her generation knew the impact of, but didn't have a name for, intergenerational trauma.

My mum, Maxine, and her siblings became the third generation who experienced forms of removal from their family. This impacted their safety, self-confidence and family connections. Maxine was raised by her dad and Nan Tucker, but she was also placed in a convent with her sister Barb, as teenagers. Mum carried this legacy of trauma into her adult life but found courage and strength in community. Like her grandmother, and Theresa and Margaret before her, Maxine had charisma; people looked to her for wisdom and assistance. Mum's career started in her mother's footsteps: in foster care. She loved listening to and helping people, in hairdressing, Aboriginal education, Aboriginal foster care, Aboriginal housing and Aboriginal Affairs. Although it was a tough gig, her focus was always on community and family, redirecting the family path so that the next generation didn't experience the same level of trauma. She wanted us to have confidence, knowledge and security in who we were as Aboriginal people. She always said, 'don't forget where you come from, and who you are'.

As the fifth generation of first-born daughters, my role in this project has been to continue being the voice for my foremothers and to keep their stories alive. I inherited this project from my mother, who passed over into the Dreamtime in 2007. We have been trying to get this book back into the hands of readers for nearly 25 years, and sometimes it seemed impossible. But when I was discouraged, these strong women in my family found ways to encourage me, through our spiritual connection. After Mum passed away, she used to visit me in my dreams to show me what I needed to do. One night, she brought Nana Mollie and Nan Tucker with her, and they sat down at a table across from me. Even though they didn't say a word, I knew then that it was my cultural obligation to keep their stories alive, to keep them present and to honour their work. Sharing the voices of past generations keeps culture strong, which is why we are publishing *If Everyone Cared Enough*, in Nan Tucker's own words. I am proud to play my part in this family story.

Tania Rossi (nee Burns)
Naarm/Melbourne, 2024

Acknowledgements

I would like to thank Initiatives of Change Australia, being the keepers of and protecting Nan's story for years and for being so co-operative with this process. Thank you for returning this book to her family.

Thank you to Aunty Maxine Briggs, for spending time and sharing archives in the State Library of Victoria with me, guiding me in the right direction with contacts and sharing some stories of Nan.

Thanks also to Marcus Hughes, who was the one to lead us to the National Library of Australia. Without you, Marcus, we would probably still be looking for a publisher. Thank you from the bottom of my heart.

And Jennifer Jones, what can I say? If it wasn't for you, this book would not be here today. I have been truly honored to work with you; your willingness to go above and beyond astounds me, your unselfishness and beautiful, humble nature is truly amazing. I know my Nan would have loved you. Thank you from the very bottom of my heart; you have helped me to fulfil my mum's wishes and have our Grandmother's voice reclaimed.

Tania Rossi

This project began in 1998 with the support of an Australian Postgraduate Award, hosted by the University of Adelaide. Initial progress was then enabled by the late Lorna White and the co-operation of Initiatives of Change Australia. I would like to thank the staff at La Trobe University for their legal advice and administrative support. This project would not have proceeded further without the support and enthusiasm of the late Maxine Barr and her daughter Tania Rossi. Our shared aim was and is to honour and preserve the memory and legacy of Margaret Tucker, a national treasure.

Jennifer Jones

Three generations of Margaret Tucker's family commemorating 80 years since the Cummeragunja Walk-Off, Cummeragunja, 2019

Picture Credits

Dennis Mayor, *Old Morago Homestead*, 1975, *If Everyone Cared* by Margaret Tucker (Sydney: Ure Smith, 1977), nla.cat-vn2376465, Courtesy Dennis Mayor

Theresa Clements and Her Four Daughters, supplied by Tania Rossi

Dennis Mayor, *Elm Trees at Moonahculla*, *If Everyone Cared* by Margaret Tucker (Sydney: Ure Smith, 1977), nla.cat-vn2376465, Courtesy Dennis Mayor

Dennis Mayor, *The Edward River*, *If Everyone Cared* by Margaret Tucker (Sydney: Ure Smith, 1977), nla.cat-vn2376465, Courtesy Dennis Mayor

Dennis Mayor, *The Murray River*, *If Everyone Cared* by Margaret Tucker (Sydney: Ure Smith, 1977), nla.cat-vn2376465, Courtesy Dennis Mayor

Theresa Clements and Her Four Daughters, supplied by Tania Rossi

Mollie as a Bride, supplied by Tania Rossi

Margaret Tucker and Her Sisters, supplied by Tania Rossi

Louise Carbines, 'Memories Hold a Fragile History', *The Age*, 20 January 1984

Brendon Kelson, *Bimbadeen College (detail) Formerly Domestic Training Home for Aboriginal Girls*, 1996, nla.cat-vn2306406

MHNSW StAC: NRS-4346-1-[9/5879B]-1-16 *Cootamundra Training Home for Girls—Dormitory*, Museum of History NSW

Margaret Tucker, Manuscript of *If Everyone Cared*, 1970s, MS 8704, nla.cat-vn326710

Billy and Jack Ingram, *If Everyone Cared* by Margaret Tucker (Sydney: Ure Smith, 1977), nla.cat-vn2376465

Margaret and Mollie, supplied by Tania Rossi

Mollie and Family, supplied by Tania Rossi

Portrait of Margaret, supplied by Tania Rossi

Dennis Mayor, *Margaret Planting a Tree*, 1964, Courtesy Dennis Mayor

Margaret with Her MBE, supplied by Tania Rossi

Margaret in New Zealand, supplied by Tania Rossi

Margaret at Her Mother's Grave, supplied by Tania Rossi

Margaret Tucker and Tania Rossi, supplied by Tania Rossi

Family Commemorating 80 Years since the Cummerajunga Walk-Off, supplied by Tania Rossi

Bibliography

Broome, Richard. *Aboriginal Victorians: A History since 1800.* Crows Nest, N.S.W.: Allen & Unwin, 2005.

Dent, Eric, and Craig Randall. 'Moral Re-Armament: Toward a Better Understanding of the Society–Corporation Relationship before the Emergence of 'Corporate Social Responsibility'.' *Journal of Management History* (2020).

Gathogo, Julius M. 'Nahashon Ngare Rukenya and the Moral Re-Armament in Kenya: The Turning Point and the Post Mau-Mau War Reconstruction (1959–1970).' *Studia Historiae Ecclesiasticae* 44, no. 2 (07/18 2018): 1–16

Goodall, Heather. *Invasion to Embassy.* Sydney: Allen and Unwin, 1996.

Grimshaw, Patricia, and Peter Sherlock. 'One Woman's Concerns for Social Justice: The Letters of Helen Baillie to Farnham Maynard, 1933–1936 '. Chap. 5 in *Anglo-Catholicism in Melbourne: Papers to Mark the 150th Anniversary of St Peter's Eastern Hill 1846–1996*, edited by Colin Holden, 85–98. Parkville, Vic.: University of Melbourne, Department of History, 1997.

Jones, Jennifer. *Black Writers White Editors: Episodes of Collaboration and Compromise in Australian Publishing History.* Melbourne: Australian Scholarly Publishing, 2009.

Lean, Garth. *Frank Buchman: A Life.* London: Constable and Company Limited, 1985.

Luttwak, Edward. 'Franco-German Reconciliation: The Overlooked Role of the Moral Re-Armament Movement.' In *Religion, the Missing Dimension of Statecraft*, edited by Douglas Johnston and Cynthia Sampson. Oxford: Oxford University Press, 1994.

Price, Jennifer. 'New News Old News: A Sociophonetic Study of Spoken Australian English in News Broadcast Speech.' *AAA: Arbeiten aus Anglistik und Amerikanistik* 33, no. 2 (2008): 285–310.

Tucker, Margaret. If Everyone Cared. Sydney: Ure Smith, 1977.

Published by National Library of Australia Publishing
Canberra ACT 2600

ISBN: 9781922507488

First edition published by Ure Smith in 1977

The National Library of Australia acknowledges Australia's First Nations Peoples—the First Australians—as the Traditional Owners and Custodians of this land and gives respect to the Elders—past and present—and through them to all Australian Aboriginal and Torres Strait Islander people.

Cover image: Dennis Mayor, *Studio Portrait of Margaret Tucker*, c.1976, H2019.87/4, State Library of Victoria, Courtesy Dennis Mayor

Publisher: Lauren Smith
Managing editor: Amelia Hartney
Designer: Jenna Lee
Image coordinator: Madeleine Warburton
Printed in Australian by Ligare on FSC®-certified paper.

Find out more about NLA Publishing at nla.gov.au/national-library-publishing.

A catalogue record for this book is available from the National Library of Australia